MW01060191

# Ethnicity in Michigan
# Issues and People

DISCOVERING THE PEOPLES OF MICHIGAN
Arthur W. Helweg and Linwood H. Cousins, Series Editors

*Ethnicity in Michigan: Issues and People*
Jack Glazier, Arthur W. Helweg

*French Canadians in Michigan*
John P. DuLong

*African Americans in Michigan*
Lewis Walker, Benjamin C. Wilson, Linwood H. Cousins

*Albanians in Michigan*
Frances Trix

---

*Discovering the Peoples of Michigan* is a series of publications examining the state's rich multicultural heritage. The series makes available an interesting, affordable, and varied collection of books that enables students and lay readers to explore Michigan's ethnic dynamics. A knowledge of the state's rapidly changing multicultural history has far-reaching implications for human relations, education, public policy, and planning. We believe that *Discovering the Peoples of Michigan* will enhance understanding of the unique contributions that diverse and often unrecognized communities have made to Michigan's history and culture.

# Ethnicity in Michigan
## Issues and People

*Jack Glazier* • *Arthur W. Helweg*

Michigan State University Press

*East Lansing*

Copyright © 2001 by Jack Glazier and Arthur W. Helweg

⊖ The paper used in this publication meets the minimum requirements
of ANSI/NISO Z39.48-1992 (R 1997) (Permanence of Paper)

Michigan State University Press
East Lansing, Michigan 48823-5202
Printed and bound in the United States of America

07 06 05 04 03 02 01 00   1 2 3 4 5 6 7 8 9 0

LIBRARY OF CONGRESS CATALOGING-IN-PUBLICATION DATA
Glazier, Jack.
Ethnicity in Michigan : issues and people / Jack Glazier, Arthur W. Helweg.
p. cm. — (Discovering the peoples of Michigan)
ISBN 0-87013-581-3 (alk. paper)
1. Minorities—Michigan—History. 2. Minorities—Michigan—Social conditions.
3. Immigrants—Michigan—History. 4. Immigrants—Michigan—Social conditions.
5. Ethnicity—Michigan. 6. Michigan—Ethnic relations. 7. Michigan—Emigration and immigration.
8. Michigan—Social conditions. I. Helweg, Arthur Wesley, 1940– II. Title. III. Series.
F575.A1 G57 2000
305.8'009774—dc21
2001000079

*Discovering the Peoples of Michigan.* The editors wish
to thank the Kellogg Foundation for their generous support.

Cover design by Ariana Grabec-Dingman
Book design by Sharp Des!gns, Inc.

Cover painting by Charles Lanman. *The Lasselle Farm on the River Raisin, Monroe, Michigan.*
Private Collection. Photo courtesy of the Monroe County Historical Association.

Visit Michigan State University Press on the World Wide Web at:
*www.msupress.msu.edu*

*This book is dedicated to Hugh Tinker—*

*scholar, mentor, and friend—*

*and to the memory of George Eaton Simpson.*

## ACKNOWLEDGMENTS

*Discovering the Peoples of Michigan* is a series of publications that resulted from the cooperation and effort of many individuals. The people recognized here are not a complete representation, for the list of contributors is too numerous to mention. However, credit must be given to Jeffrey Bonevich, who worked tirelessly with me on contacting people as well as researching and organizing material. He read and reread, checked and rechecked, and continually kept in contact with contributors. He also researched and compiled Appendices A and B.

The initial idea for this project came from Mary Erwin, but I must thank Fred Bohm, director of the Michigan State University Press, for seeing the need for this project, for giving it his strong support, and for making publication possible. Also, the tireless efforts of Keith Widder and Elizabeth Demers, senior editors at Michigan State University Press, were vital in bringing DPOM to fruition. Keith put his heart and soul into this series, and his dedication was instrumental in its success.

Otto Feinstein and Germaine Strobel of the Michigan Ethnic Heritage Studies Center patiently and willingly provided names for contributors and constantly gave this project their tireless support.

My late wife, Usha Mehta Helweg, was the initial editor. She meticulously went over manuscripts. Her suggestions and advice were crucial. Initial typing, editing, and formatting were also done by Majda Seuss, Priya Helweg, and Carol Nickolai.

The maps were drawn by Fritz Seegers while the graphics showing ethnic residential patterns in Michigan were done by the Geographical Information Center (GIS) at Western Michigan University under the directorship of David Dickason.

Russell Magnaghi must also be given special recognition for his willingness to do much more than be a contributor. He provided author contacts as well as information to the series' writers. Other authors and organizations provided comments on other aspects of the work. There are many people that were interviewed by the various authors who will remain anonymous. However, they have enabled the story of their group to be told. Unfortunately, their names are not available, but we are grateful for their cooperation.

Most of all, this work is a tribute to the writers who patiently gave their time to write and share their research findings. Their contributions are noted and appreciated. To them goes most of the gratitude.

ARTHUR W. HELWEG, *Series Co-editor*

# Contents

# Issues in Ethnicity

*Jack Glazier*

A t a time of heightened consciousness about ethnicity, the publication of a series of small volumes on the many ethnic groups that have helped shape the history of a culturally diverse state such as Michigan is altogether fitting. Entering the new millennium, Americans of the most disparate backgrounds have reason to reflect on the meanings of regional, state, and national identities, and their relationships to the specific cultures from which they derive. While many occasions prompt such consideration, the turn of the twenty-first century focuses some of these reflections. Just as 1900 arrived in the midst of an immense eastern and southern European immigration to the United States, the year 2000 likewise dawned as the face of the American nation continued to change with the steady arrival of another wave of immigration that began in 1965.[1] Unlike the early years of the twentieth century, its last years brought mostly Asian, Latin American, and Caribbean peoples to the United States. Except for the four decades of highly restricted immigration between 1924 and 1965, the United States has been the destination of many millions of newcomers. Of the approximately sixty million immigrants to the United States since the birth of the Republic, some forty million entered the country in the twentieth century.[2]

Americans of European backgrounds, Asian Americans, and Hispanic Americans represent their ethnic experience in diverse ways. Their interpretations depend on the decisive choices that they or their forbears exercised in coming to the United States and on the nature of their encounter with the new country. African Americans, by contrast, were unwilling arrivals, sundered from their communities by enslavement and held in that state by the cruelest of coercive measures. Even after Emancipation, African Americans continued for decades in caste-like subordination. These Americans provide another example of the meanings that distinct cultural heritages bring to the backdrop of history and the contemporary American scene. In this instance, cultural distinctiveness is reinforced in complex ways through its association with skin color, or racial difference. American Indians, likewise, are a special case. They are indigenes, conquered in what historian James Axtell has called, "the invasion within."[3] Politically conscious American Indians caught up in the rhetoric and acts of resistance often represent ethnicity as a form of opposition that reflects a highly charged history.

The authors of the specialized volumes in the series will convey to us the voices of individual ethnic groups in Michigan. They will, moreover, offer their own understandings and interpretations of particular styles of ethnicity amid the pluralism of the broader American culture that defines us as a people.

In this essay, I present some of the major concerns in the study of ethnicity as these are delineated in the work of social scientists, particularly anthropologists and sociologists. At the outset, it is important to state explicitly what is meant by the term "ethnicity." Anthropologists, especially, have examined the customary lifeways—the cultures—of many different groups of people on every continent. Such groups often lived in small-scale, seemingly homogeneous communities sometimes designated as "folk societies," or "tribes," where the universe of social action is generally confined to people within the same cultural tradition. In their political activity as well, little account need be taken of other cultural groups. The term "ethnic," while certainly connoting the idea of a shared tradition and value system, including a common religion, generally is not applied to the people of these culturally undifferentiated communities. Rather, ethnicity refers to distinctive cultural patterns within the pluralism of the modern nation-state. An ethnic group exists as one among several such groups within a single, complex, political order. Indeed, "tribes" and "folk societies" are now best regarded in the past tense, owing to their thoroughgoing incorporation into the nation-state where they now exist as ethnic groupings. One need only consider the contributions to this series on Michigan's cultural mosaic—the prevailing metaphor for ethnic America. Each ethnic group, marked by characteristic histories and customs, does not stand off in isolation but exists as part of a larger political whole. Examples of ethnic pluralism within a single political system abound: the Sinhalese and Tamil of Sri Lanka; the Kamba, Kikuyu, and Luo of Kenya; the Igbo, Yoruba, and Hausa of Nigeria; the Flemish and Walloons of Belgium; the Slovenians, Serbs, Croatians, Montenegrins, and Albanians of the former Yugoslavia. Such illustrations could be easily multiplied, but the point is clear. Modern states, with few exceptions, enclose within their boundaries a plurality of cultures, or ethnic groups. Both subjectively and objectively, ethnic group membership marks the group as exclusive, defined by its distinct practices, beliefs, and shared values. Members of an ethnic group are conscious of "belonging," or, their identification with a particular community is defined by culture, language, and history. Correspondingly, those outside the ethnic group also define the insiders by these same markers.

Shared history and common language as components of the definition of ethnicity bear some attention. The sense of group history, often articulated as a collective struggle against other groups, helps to define social boundaries and enhances one's ethnic identification. With language and culture, including religion, consciousness of a common past solidifies an ethnic group and adds to the salience of ethnicity in shaping one's identity. Taken together, culture, history, and language represent compelling group emblems that can motivate action and solidify a particular community while distinguishing it from all others. When coupled with strong attachments to particular territories, these symbols can sharply focus ethnic nationalist spirit, often spurring ethnic groups to seek political autonomy. Despite some periodic rumblings, quests for political independence are only a marginal aspect of ethnic issues in the United States.

Elsewhere, the territorial claims of ethnic groups are a volatile component of political behavior. We need only consider the resurfacing of ethnic feeling and the accompanying sense of nationhood in eastern Europe since the collapse of communism. Long held in check by Communist governments, powerful ethnic sentiments led to warfare and undermined the fragile political integrity of multiethnic nations such as Yugoslavia. Setting the stage for armed conflict, the dissolution of the Soviet Union into an array of internally differentiated ethnic states likewise precipitated violent outbreaks. Other examples of political instability stemming from a deep ethnic feeling (tied to claims for political autonomy) readily come to mind, such as the Kurds and the Palestinians. To invoke an apt metaphor, each nation-state now threatened by burgeoning ethnic sentiments that are tied to a perception of past and current political wrongs represents a "cauldron of ethnicity."[4] In sum, shared history and culture, bound together by the glue of common language, circumscribe an exclusive group that, under certain conditions, can become an active and separatist political force.

In the United States, members of various ethnic groups also share a distinctive language, at least historically. Here, the perpetuation of that language within a particular group is variable and problematic. Joshua Fishman points out how rapidly knowledge of the ethnic language by the second generation (the first American-born generation) has fallen away. Between 1940 and 1960, Fishman describes "sharp losses" (fifty percent or more) in the number of people claiming competence in Norwegian, Swedish, German, Czech, Slovak, Slovenian, and Finnish. He records "moderate losses" in Danish, French, Hungarian, Russian, Lithuanian, Romanian, Yiddish, and Portuguese.[5] He notes the important underlying reasons for this trend: "Economic and educational mobility within the mainstream counteract intergenerational linguistic and ethnic continuity."[6]

The loss of the vernacular for an ethnic group has important implications for the maintenance and continuity of ethnic traditions. Through language, a people within a particular cultural tradition encodes the many nuances and subtleties of their distinctive experience. By expressing the unique tonalities of its culture through a native language, an ethnic group defines itself as unique, an exclusive cultural community distinguished from all others. Full cultural participation is dependent on speaking the language. If competence in the use of a native language attenuates over the generations, as it has among European-derived ethnics in the United States, then an important boundary disappears, thereby reducing the distinctiveness of the ethnic group. Richard Alba has observed that, "A minority language can be kept alive only when there is a critical mass of speakers to provide occasions for regular use and to socialize a new generation. For the languages brought by European immigrants, such conditions appear to be dissolving."[7] He goes on to note that high rates of marriage across ethnic lines also augur badly for the flourishing of mother tongues since language continuity is linked to intra-ethnic marriage.[8]

Tendencies toward ethnic nationalism are also undermined by these linguistic trends. In view of the high rate of immigration to the United States from such areas as Latin America, public support of native language use is a lively political issue. Some observers warn of the dangers of creating the cultural and political polarities that have divided French- and English-speaking areas of Canada, to name but one example close to home. Not surprisingly, bilingualism in the United States excites considerable passion about whether the use of vernacular languages should be supported by schools and other public institutions. Wherever one stands on the contemporary debate concerning bilingual education, native language competence remains an important indicator of the depth and significance of ethnic affiliation here and elsewhere.

Many Americans strenuously claim an ethnic heritage and define their basic identities in terms of a specific cultural background. Leaving aside for a moment questions about the scope of these ethnic expressions—the extent to which they actually organize the daily lives and shape the values of ethnic claimants—their sheer pervasiveness in American life can hardly be doubted.

Expressions of ethnicity in the form of ethnic festivals, ethnic studies programs at colleges and universities, ethnic cuisines (which are often the central focus of ethnic festivals), and various other public proclamations of the value of a distinct ethnic allegiance are everywhere at hand. They have suffused our national experience to such an extent over the past thirty years that it is sometimes difficult to imagine a time when this was not the case. Daily encounters with such expressions include the purchase of foods at a Middle East bakery or an Italian market, or in the now common "ethnic foods" aisle of a large grocery store. Ethnic consciousness reaches into many domains of popular culture. Even those ubiquitous vehicles of self-advertisement—T-shirts, bumper stickers, and buttons—proclaim messages such as "Thank God I'm Finnish" or "Kiss Me I'm Greek." Affirmative action programs mandated by the federal government and various efforts to identify job applicants according to ethnic or racial categories are also routine features of contemporary life, further reinforcing in our national consciousness an almost hyperawareness of ethnicity. We are also cognizant of the new practical rewards ethnic affiliation may bring beyond the psychological satisfaction of embracing a highly particular cultural identity that separates one from the homogenizing tendencies of mass society, including globalization.

Before what has been termed the "ethnic revival" of the 1960s, many ethnic groups, particularly those of European origin, either endorsed or simply acquiesced to the prevailing American value on assimilation, represented by the familiar image of the melting pot. The great eastern and southern European immigration wave from the 1880s until the outbreak of World War I brought millions of newcomers to these shores. Their adjustment to American society set them on a course that made retention of their old country cultures extremely difficult.[9]

Whether attending Americanization classes designed to assist the adjustment process and to prepare the immigrants for citizenship, or embarking on English lessons, many immigrants rapidly internalized dominant American values. Whatever they may have failed to adopt from American culture—their accents at the least would betray them as immigrants—their American-born children suffered far fewer limitations. Public education represented an important agent for socializing the children of immigrants into American values and tastes. The promise of upward mobility was held out, yet such mobility would propel young people into a social world vastly different from the European cultural and linguistic fixtures of the immigrant home. This discontinuity of generations implicitly devalued immigrant culture, regarded as a mode of living more appropriate to a different time and different place. The satisfactions garnered from adopting mainstream American ways demanded new styles of work and leisure, new attitudes, and, of course, a new language. At one time or another, I suspect that many American-born children of these immigrants felt a tinge of embarrassment when addressed in a European language in the presence of friends whose American roots ran much deeper than their own. These changes were adopted by the children of the European immigrants over the course of a generation, thereby sharply breaking the continuity of the European experience.

Although the cultures of Europe were by no means static, the swift generational changes marking the European ethnic encounter with the United States have been nothing short of radical. As some of their children and grandchildren—the participants in the "ethnic revival" begun in the 1960s—seek to recover the cultures of their forebears, we might well ask if these efforts have revitalized ethnicity as an active social force refiguring people's lives, or merely created a pale imitation of the original. Various observers are divided on this crucial point, but a considerable weight of opinion sets forth the latter interpretation.[10]

Accordingly, Herbert Gans, asserting that assimilation continues as an active process in this country, has developed the concept of "symbolic ethnicity." It refers to the ways people have of "feeling" ethnic, of asserting an ethnic identity without participation in ethnic institutions or the wide array of cultural practices which originally defined the ethnic group. He argues that the institutional dimension of ethnicity— ethnic neighborhoods and ethnic-based organizations performing essential functions for the cultural group—has dramatically narrowed. He says that "as the functions of ethnic cultures and groups diminish and identity becomes a primary way of being ethnic, ethnicity takes on an expressive rather than instrumental function in people's lives, becoming more of a leisure-time activity and losing its relevance . . . to earning a living or regulating family life."[11] Since the major concern is to feel ethnic, no institutional supports are necessary nor are compromises that might inhibit one's participation in the cultural mainstream. The symbols expressing ethnicity are varied and range from observing ethnic holidays to eating ethnic foods. Symbolic ethnicity, in this view,

demands little effort. Richard Konisiewicz, the Cleveland mayor's liai-
son for ethnic and international affairs in the early 1990s, observed that,
"While language and genealogy may be lost or forgotten in the process
of assimilation, foods are still made the old way."[12]

Ethnic gastronomy is a particularly interesting aspect of symbolic
ethnicity because it is emblematic of how ethnic cultures in the United
States have lost their exclusiveness. Amid a continuing adoption of
mainstream American culture, a decline in the institutional basis of
ethnicity, and a loss of ethnic language competence, group boundaries
that originally delineated an exclusive membership have atrophied.
Ethnic symbols then diffuse outward, easily appropriated by anyone
who may choose them, including, of course, people claiming other ethnic backgrounds. You need not be Italian to march in the Columbus
Day parade nor Irish to participate in the St. Patrick's Day celebration.
In New York, advertising billboards at one time showed a smiling black
or Asian child and proclaimed, "You don't have to be Jewish to like
Levi's rye bread." One can maintain the dietary laws of Judaism while
enjoying Chinese food in one of New York's kosher Chinese restaurants.
Ethnic symbols abound on Shrove Tuesday, otherwise know as Paczki
Day in the Detroit area. A paczki is a Polish specialty, a kind of jelly
doughnut, traditionally consumed in large quantities on the day before
the onset of Lent, when sweets and other favored items should be given
up. Prior to a recent Lenten season, some Polish American callers to the
WJR morning program in Detroit indicated they had risen very early to
purchase several dozen doughnuts at their favorite bakeries in Detroit
and Hamtramck to share with non-Polish coworkers, to acquaint them
with this aspect of Polish culture. A pastiche of ethnic elements can
emerge, as in a hotel restaurant in Pennsylvania. Called the Captain's
Table, the restaurant features neither a seafood menu nor a nautical
decor, but a menu of pasta and other Italian specialties in a room of
high-backed chairs, glowing torches mounted on the stone walls, and a
large stone fireplace in what otherwise passed for medieval European
ambiance. If this were not enough, a sign at the exit urges patrons to
"ask about our catering service—luaus and bar mitzvahs our specialty."

Many questions thus arise about the substance and vitality of ethnicity in Michigan and the United States. Ethnicity, in its many aspects,

is part of human culture and thus subject to change. The several components of ethnicity may wax or wane in importance since they are neither fixed nor resistant to historical processes.

The case of American Indians, like that of the European ethnics in America, is illustrative. Prior to the arrival of Europeans in the New World, the many native peoples of the Americas constituted diverse cultural groupings speaking many different languages, each belonging to one of the six great super-families of American Indian languages. Considerable linguistic diversity paralleled political and economic diversity, further differentiating one society from another. The term "Indian," bestowed on native peoples by Europeans, simply conflated many different, politically distinct cultures under this single rubric. The designation "Indian" was a European convenience, a conceit born of geographic error. It lacked any psychological reality for those so labeled, for their identifications lay with their particular societies. "Indian," in short, is a colonial creation. Yet in time, the term gained salience as a supra-ethnic designation once native peoples developed a consciousness of joint grievance against agents of European expansion and a determination to act on a common interest believed to transcend cultural boundaries.

American history offers a number of pertinent examples of cross-ethnic, politico-religious movement among American Indians. The American Indian Movement (AIM) represents a particularly visible manifestation of this supra-tribal unity organized around a set of collective complaints against the government. AIM's best known resistance effort is its takeover at Wounded Knee, South Dakota, in 1973, the site of the 1890 massacre of Lakota by a cavalry detachment. Wounded Knee, in 1973, focused both on Lakota and non-Lakota Indian protest, as American Indians from numerous tribal groups made the Wounded Knee action their own. AIM, moreover, sought to construct "a universalistic Indian religion to legitimatize its pan-Indian ambitions," although the religion was essentially Oglala Lakota.[13] Further, a "standard narrative," historically suspect but politically potent, of the American Indian has emerged, alleging many common themes and elements across all cultures of native North America.[14]

The federal government plays a critical role in defining who is an

Indian. That this definition has changed over time—toward more lib-
eral specifications—is yet another example of the shifts that ethnicity
regularly undergoes at various historical junctures. As cultural and
political attitudes toward American Indians are transformed, the number of people so identifying themselves correspondingly changes. Thus,
the 1980 census shows a seventy-five percent rise in the American
Indian population over the figure reported in 1970.[15] Obviously, some-
thing other than natural increase is at work here. The native population
(American Indian, Inuit, and Aleut), according to the 1990 census, again
rose sharply, increasing forty-five percent over the 1980 figures.[16] While
this figure is thirty percent under the 1970-80 increase, it still represents
an astonishing growth in population, dramatically higher than what
one might expect from natural increase. The Indian population of
Michigan likewise surged by 38.9 percent, thus nearly coinciding with
the national figures. To put these numbers in the proper context, it
should be noted that at approximately four percent natural increase
per year, Kenya is experiencing a veritable demographic explosion with
one of the highest rates of population growth in the world. Following
the 1990 census, an article in the *New York Times* summed up some of
the reasons for these changes: "As American society becomes more
accepting and admiring of the Indian heritage, and as governments set
aside contracts and benefits for tribe members, an increasing number
of Indians . . . feel freer to assert their identities."[17]

Leaving aside the historical similarities and differences between
native peoples of North America, it is clear that AIM as a political organization can more effectively build its strength and base of support
among various Indian peoples by emphasizing putative historical, religious, and cultural bonds between constituent units. In this instance,
new ethnic identifications and definitions more effectively serve political functions by mobilizing people to seek changes in government
policies, especially those of the Bureau of Indian Affairs. As the *New
York Times* article suggests, economic provisions earmarked for one or
another ethnic category render ethnicity particularly useful.

If it pays material reward, then ethnic consciousness may become a
critical part of one's public self-identification. Ethnic frictions also may
ensue, however, when some groups fail to become beneficiaries of

government-sponsored rewards or programs. If membership in a particular group defines a set of collective rights vis-à-vis some good, then
an ethnic body may in some contexts represent another kind of interest group serving its members in much the same way as a labor union,
a professional organization, or a lobby. Although a decidedly unro-
mantic aspect of ethnicity, interest group organization and political
stratagems played out along ethnic lines nonetheless highlight the way
in which public or institutional policy can actively promote heightened
ethnic consciousness that in turn can positively reinforce that policy.

Efforts on many college campuses in support of "multiculturalism"
(an omnibus term covering cultural diversity in faculties and curricula)
also explicitly repudiate the older emphasis on America as a melting pot
and provide a particularly stark example of the political uses of ethnicity.
In considering the multicultural movement on campus, the *Cleveland
Plain Dealer* reported Shelby Steele's sharp observation: "I think it's used
as a power term. Behind it, you usually have people lined up demanding
things; separate black studies, Asian studies, women's studies. They are
usually making demands on the system, and the focus is on whatever
their power needs are, rather than any exposition of the culture."[18]

The case of the Chinese in the United States presents yet another
example of the dynamics of ethnicity within the broader context of
American society. Bernard Wong provides an ethnographic portrait of
New York's Chinatown that points up numerous differences in the
meanings and uses of ethnicity for different groups within the New York
Chinese community. Two of the more important are the old overseas
Chinese and the Chinese Americans, either American-born or naturalized. The older group inhabits a world limited to Chinatown, where
they live and work. Their contact with the American mainstream takes
place in their ethnic businesses such as Chinese restaurants. Their
significant social networks are Chinese, centering on relationships with
kin, friends, or people from the same village. They actively participate
in Chinese holidays and other observances and have a limited knowledge of English, relying instead on the Chinese press, which itself is
highly chauvinistic.[19] They are the denizens of a vigorous ethnic enclave
full of viable Chinese institutions that influence every dimension of
their lives.

By contrast, the younger generation of Chinese Americans disavows ethnic insularity in favor of full participation in American society, especially since legal barriers have fallen. Chinese Americans do not necessarily live in Chinatown. Often in the professions, or otherwise well-educated, naturalized Chinese and American-born Chinese have encountered various illegal discriminatory obstacles. Unlike the older generation indifferent to political participation or to the wider currents of American society, Chinese Americans have found inspiration in the attempts of black and Hispanic Americans to press for full social and civic participation. In effect, they have formed what Wong calls an ethnic "pressure group" which can perform both the expressive function of "instilling ethnic pride" and the purely instrumental function of gaining "their share from the city, state, and federal government."[20] In this respect, ethnicity as interest, in the political and economic sense, once again serves the same utilitarian functions as the American Indian Movement.

The Chinese American stake in cultivating ethnic pride is more than a singular instance of a particular cultural group struggling with a double identity. It encapsulates the dilemma faced by many ethnic groups in the United States. Deliberate efforts to promote such pride are full of anxiety and questioning. These attempts imply at least a tacit recognition that ethnic continuity is not assured in the United States for various and complex reasons defying simple formulas. It would be historically myopic to ignore the destructive effects of exclusion, legal and extralegal, of racial and ethnic groups from the mainstream, and the fundamental contradictions this poses to national ideals. But enforced exclusion is only part of a complicated story still unfolding. The older Chinese are hardly targets of efforts to instill pride because they entertain no doubts about the validity of their customary beliefs and styles of living that penetrate every dimension of their social existence. They are, in other words, pervasively rather than situationally ethnic. If anything, the older Chinese are intensely ethnocentric, unmoved to celebrate identity in a self-conscious fashion and untroubled by any doubts about the validity and superiority of their customary beliefs and activities.

Put simply, how can ethnic groups simultaneously maintain continuity in their cultural traditions, including the continuation of the native language, while also participating in the broad spectrum of American political, economic, and social life? This has proven to be a nearly insurmountable challenge to many ethnic groups, recognizing as they have that a quest for education, economic improvement, social mobility—in short the pursuit of particular goals enshrined in the American value system—would bring heavy costs to the cause of ethnic continuity. For good or ill, the realization of these values historically occurred by spurning, or at least suspending, outside the home the most visible emblems of ethnic affiliation—distinctive language, dress, and the like. Robert A. Rockaway's study of Detroit's Jewish community up to 1914 aptly concludes by observing that the tension between participation in American society and the maintenance of ethnic identity never achieved a resolution.[21] In summing up the matter regarding Jewish immigrants in New York early in the twentieth century, Irving Howe offers less equivocal remarks that also bear on the experience of other ethnic communities: "On behalf of its sons, the East Side was prepared to commit suicide; perhaps it did."[22] Immigrants made enormous cultural sacrifices to accelerate the social and economic mobility of their children.

Some groups have managed with considerable success to remain apart from mainstream American culture and to mitigate the processes to which Howe refers, but only through very unusual strategies that most ethnic groups have rejected. Ethnic enclaves such as the various Chinatowns of the largest American cities, or the Hasidic communities of Brooklyn are cases in point. Whether voluntary or reactive to harshly discriminatory practices or some combination of the two, such enclaves can provide cultural insulation, especially if they can manage some degree of economic self-sufficiency. Language and culture, otherwise changed by those leaving the ethnic enclave, could thus find a preserve bearing much more than a superficial resemblance to their Old World origins. Ethnic isolates can also emerge in rural areas, where self-sufficient farming distant from large cities can sequester unique cultural groups.

For example, the Amish communities ranging across the American Middle West attempt to maintain their continuity through a deliberate turning away from particular social and technical aspects of the American mainstream—public education, social security, familiar clothing, electricity, automobiles, and the like. The documentary film, *The Amish: Not to Be Modern*, clearly illustrates these patterns among the Ohio Amish. Their efforts to maintain distance from the world yield only partial dividends since some young people leave their communities for city life and all that it entails. Only by having many children do Amish families cut their losses and ensure cultural continuity. Even with a high degree of social isolation, the Amish have not found it possible to keep all cultural currents at bay, partly because of their proximity to non-Amish communities and the necessity of forging economic linkages through off-farm labor or marketing their farm products to people outside the Amish community.

Of course, de jure exclusion and separation, augmented by racialism and ethnic bias historically, served to enforce social separation on particular groups—blacks, Asians, American Indians and, for a briefer period, eastern and southern European ethnics. American blacks, especially, long noted the discrepancy between broader cultural values on opportunity, personal economic betterment, education and civic participation, on the one hand, and the social and legal obstacles blocking the realization of these values, on the other. This kind of contradiction—or what anthropologists and sociologists have termed relative deprivation—propelled the modern civil rights movement for the elimination of legal and customary impediments to full participation in American society. The 1960s also produced various expressions of black nationalism, emphasizing political and cultural bonds between black Americans and Africans, phrased in the idiom of colonial resistance. When social institutions, ranging from schools, to businesses, to labor unions, failed Americans of African descent who sought to realize the mainstream values they had internalized, many young people developed a heightened black consciousness drawing on African symbols, including that of anticolonialism. Alex Haley's *Roots* stirred popular interest in the African past and, particularly, in historical relationships between black American and West African peoples. These cultural interests punctuated by personal identification with Africa in turn stimulated Americans of European background to rehyphenate themselves in the broad effort to revitalize ethnicity in the contentious political climate of the late 1960s.

Black Americans also developed an interest in African arts and crafts, clothing (which could easily be adopted as one's own), and learning African languages, particularly the East African lingua franca, Kiswahili (Swahili). It matters little that black Americans overwhelmingly derive from West African populations that speak languages very different from those of East Africa. Here, too, as in the other instances cited, ethnicity and its varied and shifting symbolism are firmly bound to the political purposes they often serve.

This observation does not gainsay the psychological functions that powerful new symbols or rearrangements of old ones can hold for individuals, nor does it minimize the historical record of brutality in the shattering of many cultural bonds, including the languages linking black Americans to Africa. Yet ethnicity as resistance or reinvention is, I suspect, paradoxical. It may be closely linked to the often uncomfortable realization among ethnic activists about how profoundly mainstream culture has influenced them.

All of this once again raises the question of the import of contemporary ethnicity in the United States in general and in Michigan in particular. Are ethnic symbols and practices enduring continuations of the traditional culture from which they are said to spring? Are they cultural badges identifying political and economic interest groups? Or are they highly selective markers, albeit psychologically meaningful ones, of a personal identity individuals wish to embrace on their own terms without compromising their participation in familiar American cultural routines that are themselves empty of ethnic content? I have suggested some of the ways social scientists have thought about these issues, but ordinary citizens as well cannot help but ponder their relevance to our national experience, both now and for the future. Thus, as Americans look back to the beginning of the twentieth century and the wave of immigration that transformed our national life, they will also look ahead as the face of America continues to undergo substantial changes through the renewal of large-scale immigration.

The character of various American cities reflects the surge of new and recent immigrants, especially from Asia and Latin America, promising to recast the culture and politics of particular areas. Miami, transformed as a result of the Cuban immigration, is one of the more dramatic examples.[23] There, ethnicity has provided a channel to upward mobility, whereas for earlier generations of European-derived groups, ethnicity often presented an obstacle to economic mobility. Elsewhere, the new immigrants are building new and growing ethnically based economies. In contrast to the four decades between the 1880s and 1920s, the immigration of Europeans now constitutes only a very small part of the current movement of peoples to the United States. The adjustment of the newcomers to their adopted country and, indeed, the country's adjustment to its increasingly diverse citizenry, either in familiar or novel ways, will provide further challenges to our various understandings of the dynamics of ethnicity and its role in American life.

# Ethnicity in Michigan

*Arthur W. Helweg*

Ethnicity is one of the most powerful social forces impinging on human behavior. People live, fight, and die to maintain their ethnicity or to ensure the survival of their ethnic community. Besides causing conflict, ethnicity can determine social ranking and define rights and duties. Ethnicity has its positive side also. It sets forth a meaning and purpose in life for a group and its members, it gives people a community to belong to, and it provides rules to live by and criteria for self and social evaluation.

An ethnic group is composed of people who share self-defined common characteristics, which usually include a mythology and/or tradition,[1] homeland, history, culture,[2] and language.[3] Inhabitants of Michigan, like all people, become part of a group or groups of people for a variety of reasons. People may identify with a community to have a sense of belonging, to have access to resources, to be protected, or to feel comfortable being with people of like mind and similar backgrounds. Membership may be voluntary, with the individual choosing membership, or ascribed by the wider society, as is the case when physical characteristics like skin color or eye shape classifies membership. One's ethnicity is determined by the particular ethnic group with whom he or she identifies.

Regardless of the motivation or basis of membership, several things must be kept in mind. Membership in an ethnic group provides a culture which gives answers to such vital questions as: What is the purpose of my life? What is right and wrong? Where do I belong? Ethnicity provides a tie to the eternal—a tradition on which to build so as to make life better for the next generation. Thus, once a person commits to a tradition, he or she does not want those values or beliefs rejected by the next generation. An individual will do whatever they deem necessary to preserve their way of life—self worth depends on it. People usually have multiple ethnicities and choose one according to the context. For example, when I am in the United States, I am a German American, but when I am in Europe, I am an American.

Ethnicity is always changing. Kathleen Conzens, in her 1990 address to the Annual Meeting of the Immigration History Society, argued that identity was analogous to a river. Like a river, ethnicity and ethnic groups change by taking on or discarding elements. One community may divide into two or more, while several groups may merge into one. As the publications in the *Discovering the Peoples of Michigan* series will show, these dynamics not only have taken place in Michigan, but are part of Michigan's current social processes.

To understand the ethnic dynamics of Michigan, Jack Glazier, in the previous essay has provided a good framework by identifying major categories of analysis, namely: (a) the unique experiences, conditions, and context by which a group entered an area, (b) the distinctive social and cultural characteristics of the community, and (c) the nature and degree of participation of a group in the host society of their new abode. It is around these themes that the following essay will be organized.

Michigan's population has undergone numerous changes since her settlement by human beings. Thus, the analysis of the state's dynamics will be discussed within the context of two major classifications. The first "From Many to One" (*E Pluribus Unum*) is subdivided into three processes:[4] (a) Pristine process, the time before Europeans arrived, (b) Frontier process, when Europeans established the fur trade and extended the conflicts of Europe to North America, and (c) Pioneering process, when people of New England and New York, followed by Europeans, settled in large numbers west of Detroit to farm. "From One to Many" (*Ex Uno Plures*) also focuses on three processes: (a) Development, when the infrastructure of roads, canals, and railroads grew along with extractive industries such as lumbering and mining, (b) Industrialization, when manufacturing became prominent, and (c) Modern, when knowledge, service-based and high technology-based organizations came to the fore.[5]

## From Many to One

People who entered Michigan to stay during the "From Many to One" period tended not to maintain as strong an ethnic distinctiveness as did people who came later, especially after the Second World War. Groups such as the Dutch and Germans formed communities, but there was an understanding that permanent settlers would adhere to the established culture, which at the time of the European influx was based primarily on English and New England Yankee ways.

### Pristine Process

Although little is known about this period, it is by far the longest as Native Americans have occupied the upper Great Lakes for the last 12,000 years. Most scholars agree that the descendants of Native Americans originated in Asia and started crossing Bering Strait roughly 14,000 years ago. Around 1000 B.C., they carried on long distance trade and adopted burial ceremonies. In the Upper Peninsula, people produced tools from copper mined on the Keweenaw Peninsula. They were possibly the first humans to make and use metal tools.

The original settlers in Michigan were the Paleo-Indians who descended from the people who crossed the Bering Strait. By the time Europeans first reached the Great Lakes in the 1620s, the Anishnabeg, meaning "original people" or "first people," had replaced the Paleo-Indians. The Ojibwa (Chippewa), Ottawa, and Potawatomi, who comprised the Anishnabeg, had migrated from the Atlantic Coast. They welcomed the first European explorers, traders, and missionaries into their villages.

Although people inhabiting the northern regions of the Great Lakes perceived of themselves as hunters at the time of European contact,

## INITIAL MIGRATION INTO AMERICA 50,000–1000 B.C.

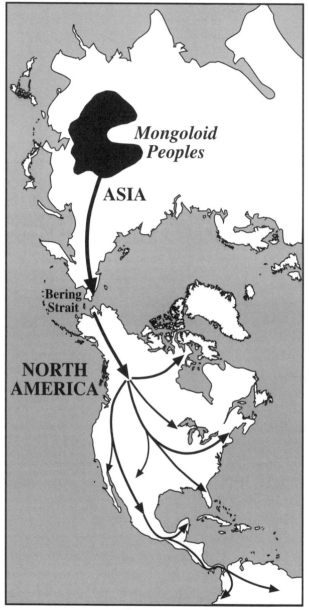

*The first people to live in Michigan descended from people who originated in Asia. Adapted from Martin Gilbert,* The Dent Atlas of American History *(London: J. M. Dent, 1993), 1.*

fishing dominated their economy. People living further south grew corn, beans, and squash, all crops first cultivated in Central America. They supplemented their livelihood by hunting and gathering.

At the beginning of the Historic period (1600 A.D.) the Anishnabeg did not identify with a tribe as we use the term today. They identified with kin group, band, totem, phratry, or a larger group. The Anishnabeg related to the group who spoke a common dialect and shared similar customs, traditions, and mythological origins. Anishnabeg men and women traced their kinship ties and clan membership through their male progenitors. Identification did not come from being a member of a tribe, but rather "from the close intimate relations of everyday life."[6]

Michigan's Native Americans were a religious people who attributed their existence to divine action. They saw and experienced spiritual entities all around them in the earth, water, and sky. Indian cosmology did not make distinctions between the animate and inanimate. Some spirits played tricks while others brought justice. The spirits, along with the plants, animals, and rocks were all part of the symbiotic whole, which included the Anishnabeg. Human beings, spirits, plants, and animals existed in mutual interactional relationships. Consequently, the Anishnabeg showed great respect for all of Creation.[7]

The Anishnabeg chose their leaders on ability and charisma rather than through elections, or heredity, and councils governed by consensus.[8] This created obstacles for the Europeans, especially in treaty negotiations, because no one individual spoke for the group as European representatives did.[9] When the Native Americans referred to the "Great White Father" they did not envision the hierarchical relationships constructed by Europeans. Many Indian communities in Michigan today continue to hold to the egalitarian ideal and still make decisions by consensus rather than by majority.

Reciprocity formed the basis for social relationships in Native American society. Marriage and gift exchange tied bands and kin groups together in networks of mutual rights and obligations, which were crucial for survival. The Anishnabeg extended generous hospitality to their kin and others, freely giving gifts and help whenever a need arose.[10] The presentation of gifts established a close relationship whereby a donor expected to receive help or support from others in his or her time of need.

Before European contact, the Native Americans of Michigan had established extensive trade networks with other Native people. Warfare existed in the form of periodic raids, not prolonged engagements, and usually the attackers did not have territorial objectives. Traveling by birch bark canoes over lakes and streams, the Anishnabeg extended their influence along dispersed social networks created by their clans and phratries throughout a large part of northeastern North America.[11] When the Europeans entered Michigan, most of Michigan's Indians were connected to the Algonquin and Huron peoples by either trade, kinship, language, and/or political alliance. They freely gave help and presents and took whatever the Europeans gave in return, interpreting the exchange within their cultural framework. With European encroachment, the Anishnabeg's identity and life style changed.

### Frontier Process

The influx of Europeans dramatically changed the identity and culture of Michigan's people. The Europeans were guided by the mercantile philosophy which led to their insatiable quest for wealth. Capitalism resulted in their audacious pursuit of profit. The white man's concept of territoriality was diametrically opposed to the Native American's concept of the forest being for all. Europeans saw the Indians as heathen who must convert to Christianity to obtain salvation. They also brought their conflicts and animosities from their homelands and involved the American indigenous population in struggles between European states.

Goods manufactured in Europe replaced products made locally, which led to Native Americans becoming dependent upon the Europeans. Consequently, the Native people lost some of their traditional skills such as pottery making. The power of European armies and their tactics eventually subjugated the indigenous population to European influence and control.

The French were the first Europeans to come to Michigan, and they claimed the land for France. The early French explorers exemplified a curiosity for the unknown, a quest for adventure, a desire to serve God and king, and a passion for wealth, all of which brought them into contact with the Native people. Merchants obtained furs from the Indians and shipped them to Europe, through Canada. Soon Roman Catholic missionaries followed and baptized Native Americans into the Christian faith. Missionaries at times played dual roles as explorer and priest. Father Jacques Marquette spread Christianity while exploring the interior of North America for France. On the other hand, Etiénne Brulé, the first Frenchman to set foot on Michigan soil in the early 1620s, had no desire to take Christianity to the Native people.

As the French presence grew in Michigan, four sub-groups of people emerged: the *coureurs de bois, voyageurs, habitants,* and *Métis.* The *coureurs de bois* lived and traded, without licenses, among the Indians far away from French civil and military authorities. *Voyageurs,* or *engagés,* transported furs and merchandise for licensed traders between Quebec and the wilderness of the western Great Lakes. They, like the *coureurs de bois,* formed marital relationships with Native women; these ties led to the creation of trade networks among their wives' kin.

The *habitants* were farmers who settled at Detroit. They grew crops on farms, which they had established on both sides of the Detroit River. These farms all had a narrow frontage on the river, extending back into the woods creating the appearance of a series of parallel ribbons. The *habitants* produced food for themselves and people working in the fur trade. They also maintained ties with Huron, Ottawa, and Potawatomi men and women living in nearby villages.

Since the early French intermarried with the Native Americans, their offspring resulted in a new ethnic group—the *Métis.* These bicultural people drew upon the ways and beliefs of both of their heritages. They served as mediators between the Europeans and Native Americans in the fur trade, in diplomatic matters concerning war and peace, and the use and settlement of land. They joined together the worlds of the Indians and the Europeans and helped both groups understand each other.[12]

After the French lost the French and Indian War (1754–1763) to the British, most French-speaking people stayed in Michigan. As Scottish, Scotch-Irish, Irish, English, and Jewish merchants entered the trade, they not only competed against the French, but they also employed many of the French to carry on their trading enterprises. Soon, the newcomers gained financial control of the trade. But the French *habitants* remained on their farms, and the *Métis* and French Canadians continued to live and work among their Native kin. The Indians persisted in the fur trade, and many of them practiced agriculture to help sustain themselves as well as European immigrants in the late eighteenth and early nineteenth centuries.

### Pioneering Process

The creation of the United States in 1776 set the stage for further immigration into Michigan. The Northwest Ordinances of 1784, 1785, and 1787 incorporated Michigan along with the future states of Ohio, Indiana, Illinois, and Wisconsin into the new American nation.[13] New settlement in Michigan was slow until after the War of 1812, but the Erie Canal in 1825 opened the floodgates. Thousands of people from New England, New York, Ohio, Pennsylvania, New Jersey, and Canada arrived by steamship in Detroit to take up residence in Michigan Territory. Many "Yankees" left the Northeast because of the declining availability and productivity of land, and the prospect of rich soil in Michigan. As the nineteenth century wore on, roads, canals, and railroads brought many more people to join French Canadians and Native Americans already living in Michigan. Michigan achieved statehood in 1837.[14]

Yankee culture emphasized individualism, family unity, and the capitalistic orientation of maximizing profits.[15] Alexis de Tocqueville observed during his visit to Michigan in 1831 that pioneers were not poor. Land was cheap, but the cost of supplies and labor was high. A new settler needed at least $150 to get started. De Tocqueville also noted the high level of knowledge possessed by new immigrants, who valued education and opposed slavery, while some espoused women's rights.[16] They brought with them a strong sense of individualism, ingenuity, equality, puritan values, mobility, and an entrepreneurial spirit. Most farmed, but others set up commercial businesses or started small industrial firms. The immigrants created an increasingly diverse economic base that stimulated growth and attracted more people to Michigan from the East and Europe.[17]

Immigrants to Michigan were mobile. Whether they came alone or with their families, most people entered Michigan through Detroit. From Detroit they made their way further inland to farmsteads where they built a small dwelling and cleared land so that they could plant crops as soon as possible. As farmers became more prosperous, they replaced their log cabins with larger Greek-revival houses.[18] After a few years, many settlers sold their improved farms and moved further west to Minnesota, Iowa, or even California. They left behind towns named after their old communities in New England or New York: Hartford, Watervliet, Rochester, Mount Morris, Bath, Utica, Albion, Ithaca, and others. Life in these villages and larger settlements such as Pontiac, Ann Arbor, and Monroe revolved around the church, town meetings, schools, stores, mills, and shops.[19]

By the middle of the nineteenth century, African Americans had established several small enclaves in Michigan, most notably in Detroit and Cass County. Some black immigrants were fugitives who had come by the Underground Railroad, but most were freed slaves. Quakers helped runaway slaves establish permanent residence in places such as Calvin Township in Cass County. Some African Americans came North after their wealthy, southern plantation owners had left provisions in their wills to free their slaves and provided money for them to move to Michigan. For example, the executors of Sampson Saunder's will bought a plot of land in Calvin Township, and by 1849 forty-six African American men, women, and children had settled there. They built a community around well-cultivated farms, comfortable houses, and eight country schoolhouses. Black teachers taught the children in four of the schools.[20] Other African American rural communities grew up in Cassopolis, Covert, and Baldwin.

Discrimination against African Americans in Michigan prevented them from voting, serving on juries, and attending white schools. In 1842, the African Americans in Detroit formed the "Colored Vigilance Committee" to "wage political and moral warfare" for civil rights. In 1843, a national convention demanding civil rights for blacks was followed by one in Michigan. African Americans tried by legal means to obtain their rights, but when a state Senate committee rejected a joint resolution to give blacks the right to vote, it expressed the prevailing sentiment in Michigan that: "Our Government is formed by, for the benefit of, and to be controlled by, the descendants of European nations, as distinguished from all other persons."[21] African Americans living in Michigan faced a long, uphill struggle to gain equality.

As the pioneers moved in, many Indians were forced off their land. The removal policies of President Andrew Jackson led to the removal or attempted removal of Native people living in Michigan. Although many Potawatomi went to Kansas and some Ottawa left for Canada, a large number of Michigan's Potawatomi, Ottawa, and Chippewa successfully resisted deportation.[22] Their determination to remain in the state ensured a continued presence of Native Americans in Michigan.

### From One to Many

Pioneers from New England and New York provided a homogeneous cultural base for Michigan's nineteenth-century immigrant population. As western Europeans settled in the state, there was enough common-ality among them, especially the Germans and the Dutch who formed ethnic enclaves to fit into the prevailing culture. As people came from other countries and labored in Michigan's lumber and mining indus-tries, they began to group, be grouped, and treated according to language and place of origin. The process of social fragmentation increased considerably when more immigrants came to work in facto-ries located near Detroit and other cities in Michigan. This in turn encouraged immigrants to retain a strong sense of ethnic identity. Also, better communication with home countries contributed to the survival of old world ethnicity.

### Development Process

After 1840 the settling of Michigan took on a different character. People emigrating from Germany and England bought farms previously owned by old-stock Americans who had moved further west or to cities. By 1890 the Germans were the most numerous foreign-born population in Michigan, numbering about 135,000. The Germans and other western Europeans primarily came from rural areas or small communities where everyone was acquainted with everyone else. They all knew

## EUROPEAN EMIGRATION TO THE U.S. 1820–1920

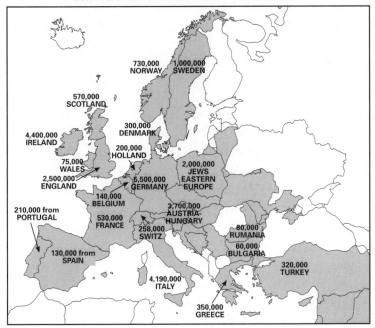

*Between 1820 and 1920 millions of people emigrated from Europe to the United States. This map reveals how many people came from different countries. Adapted from Martin Gilbert,* The Dent Atlas of American History *(London: J. M. Dent, 1993), 65.*

whom they could depend upon for help in time of need. Within the family, gender defined the division of labor and authority. Many European immigrants were not well educated and possessed few skills beyond those needed to farm. Possessing a strong sense of community, many Europeans migrated to the United States only after consultation with family and friends. Once in Michigan, relatives and friends helped new arrivals find their places in their new homeland.

A common method of immigration to Michigan was "chain migration" where one person left the homeland and took up residence in the new land. Later he sent back reports of his new home and encouraged family and others to follow. The Irish practiced this widely, and whole German villages resettled in Michigan. Some groups, such as the Dutch, kept the communities of the old country intact when they settled in Michigan. It was not long, however, before ties with their country of origin weakened.

In early years many people crossing the Atlantic Ocean found their voyage, which could last from six weeks to several months, to be a terrifying experience. They sailed in cramped, crowded cargo ships where poor ventilation, filth, overcrowding, and inadequate sanitation facilities caused great suffering.[23] Frequently passengers did not have enough food and water, which made them more susceptible to disease. It is no wonder that Joseph Ruff, a German immigrant, wrote that, "I would not wish to try the experience again." Thus, for many settlers during this period, the voyage often ensured that return was not feasible. The ties with the homeland had been broken.[24]

As transportation across the Atlantic became faster and safer, ongoing communication with the old country and the continuing influx of people from the same region reinforced the maintenance of old-world culture. Many Romanian peasants, for example, intended "to make $1,000 and return." Other later immigrants kept their ties with the home country by sending money to family and friends.

Immigrants often settled in Michigan because of choices made after they arrived in the United States. Informal hearsay or the offer of cheap land by a speculator in Michigan lands directed people to the state. As a result, immigrants forged a strong sense of individualism and self-reliance, which coincided with some of the same traits of the old-stock Americans who preceded them.

Michigan's changing economy during the second half of the nineteenth and the twentieth centuries shaped the population composition of the state and influenced ethnic dynamics. Employment opportunities in Michigan's lumber, mining, and manufacturing industries mushroomed. Lumbering thrived between 1840 and 1920. In fact, the wealth created by Michigan's "green gold," lumber, exceeded that of the "yellow gold" of the California Gold Rush. French, Irish, Canadian, and Native American woodsmen cut most of the trees harvested in the nineteenth century. Workers in the lumber towns also came from Norway, Sweden, Poland, England, Germany, Holland, Russia, Scotland, and Denmark.[25] Copper and iron mining started in the mid-1840s then virtually ceased in the mid-1940s. The workforce in this industry included Finns, English, Scots, Italians, and Germans. Iron ore production remained high until the 1930s, when the open pit mines of the West yielded more ore than Upper Peninsula mines.[26] The character of the immigrant population changed even more as Italians, Hungarians, Poles, and Middle Easterners sailed to America and continued on to Michigan.

In the Upper Peninsula, European immigrants transcended the Chippewa Indians and *Métis* as the dominant people and introduced tensions created when a place becomes more ethnically diverse. In 1850 the first major influx of miners from Cornwall arrived. By 1870, two-thirds of the mine workers in the U.P. were Cornish or Irish. The Cornish had mined copper in England, and as the mines in Cornwall declined (partly due to American competition) the Cornish who found their way to the Upper Peninsula revolutionized mining methods. They lived a tough life both in and out of the mines. In order to keep their workers, mine owners furnished housing, which resulted in the establishment of more families, churches, and schools.[27]

After the Civil War, Finnish, Swedish, and Norwegian immigrants traveled directly to the Upper Peninsula. Since their homelands could not support the growing population, letters from friends and relatives in the United States (known as "American Letters"), stories of returnees, guidebooks, and agents from mine companies, lured many people to Michigan.[28] The Scandinavians were highly educated, religiously conservative, and physically strong. They possessed meager capital but had dreams to obtain great wealth.[29]

English- and French-speaking Canadians arrived in Michigan in the middle of the nineteenth century. They worked in mining, agriculture, fishing, and domestic service. They published newspapers and participated in their churches. Germans were recruited because they worked hard. Starvation, poverty, and oppression drove many Irish to Michigan in search of employment. Within the family structure of all groups a strict division of labor based on gender existed.

Social networks growing out of ethnic identification joined miners and lumbermen together. Men who worked alongside of one another attended the same church with their families, drank at the same bar,

and lived in the same neighborhoods. Fearful of too much fraterniza-
tion between different groups, mine owners and lumber barons con-
sciously segregated ethnic groups. They separated the Cornish from the
Irish and kept the Poles apart from the Swedes. Owners followed traditional "divide and rule" tactics, using Poles, for example, as strike-
breakers when the Cornish went on strike.

Industrial Process

Population movement patterns changed as the lumbering and mining
industries declined, and manufacturing, especially the automobile
industry, grew. Rural to urban migration increased as people living on
farms realized that they could make more money working in factories.
Unemployed miners and lumberjacks moved to Detroit and other
industrial centers. When Henry Ford increased wages from $2.30 to
$5.00 per day, double the going factory rate, other manufactures soon
followed. News of the high wages spread to the far corners of Michigan,
North America, and Europe. Workers flocked to Detroit from all over
the world.

Cotton workers in the southern United States saw the boll weevil
destroy their livelihood, and they responded to recruiters, news reports,
and word-of-mouth accounts extolling the opportunities in Michigan.
Black and white families moved to Michigan and other states as part of
the Great Northern Migration—the largest internal migration in North
American history. African Americans, in large numbers, answered the
calls of labor recruiters to find work in Detroit's factories.[30] Between
1910 and 1920, Michigan's African American population rose from 17,115
to 60,082. By 1930 it was 169,452, with 120,000 residing in Detroit.[31]
Blacks also tried to escape the ramifications of the *Plessy v. Ferguson*
case where, in 1896, the United States Supreme Court upheld the prin-
ciple that segregation by race was legal.

For African Americans, the dream of equality and freedom did not
materialize. In Michigan they also faced discrimination and violence.
As early as 1863 the Faulkner incident resulted in racial conflict and
foreshadowed Detroit's future ethnic problems.[32] Resentment and tension arising from the Civil War and imposition of the draft led to anger
and frustration directed against the African American population. It

## GREAT NORTHERN MIGRATION, 1917–20

*Large numbers of African Americans and poor whites, in search of employment and freedom, moved from the South to industrial cities in the North. Adapted from Arthur W. Helweg, "Great Northern Migration," in* Encyclopedia of North American History, *consulting ed. John C. Super (New York: Marshall Cavendish, 1999), 511–13; and John H. Long, "The Great Migration: The South Moves North," in* The Settling of North America: The Atlas of the Great Migrations into North America from the Ice Age to the Present, *ed. Helen Hornbeck Tanner (New York: Macmillan), 148–49.*

was in this climate that William Faulkner, an African American male was accused of raping two white women. When a crowd came to get Faulkner, a deputy shot into the crowd killing a white man. This sparked a race riot that targeted the African American community. Federal soldiers had to be brought in to quell the violence. In 1943, even when economic conditions were good, racism provoked hate strikes and racial violence.[33] Competition, rather than cooperation, between blacks and whites for jobs, health care, housing, and leisure characterized relations between the races.

By the turn of the twentieth century, the new immigrants came to Michigan primarily from economically depressed eastern and southern Europe. They fled the deprivations caused by European industrialization and their subsequent forced removal from of their lands, to the urban industrial centers of America where jobs were available.[34] Poles became the dominant group in the Detroit area, and by 1900 they were the largest foreign-born group, numbering 66,113. By 1930, Detroit had become a multi-ethnic city with Italian-born totaling 21,711, Russian-born 11,162, Hungarian-born 9,014, Yugoslavian-born 7,576, Romanian-born 6,385, and Greek-born 6,385. Finns, Arabs, and others from the Middle East were also prominent in the Detroit metropolitan area.[35]

Ethnic groups clustered in both rural areas and the cities. By the end of the nineteenth century, a residential map of ethnic settlement in Detroit looked like a patchwork quilt.[36] Greeks, Chaldeans, and Arabs, among many others, each had their distinctive neighborhoods.[37] Ethnic clusters also formed in rural Michigan. For example, in Berrien and Van Buren Counties, before corporations started buying family farms in the 1960s, German names such as Klett, Epple, and Frazee were prominent names on mailboxes surrounding Hartford, Watervliet, and Eau Claire. Living among people who spoke the same language and came from same culture enabled thousands of immigrants to adjust to life in crowded, dirty cities or in isolated farm houses. As they shared their lives in their churches, schools, mills, shops, and streets, they helped each other nurse their sick, feed their hungry, warm their cold, celebrate their marriages, and mourn their dead.

Ethnic factors became issues in religion and politics. For example, in 1885 violence erupted on Christmas Day after the Poles felt that the German-born bishop, Caspar H. Borgess, was being unfair to them. In 1894 Polish workers digging a trench for a city water project in Detroit went on strike because they were not being paid the wage that had been promised to them. Similar incidents became a regular feature of life in Michigan.

Foreign-born and Catholic immigrants, who often crowded into urban ghettos, looked to the Democratic Party to cater to their needs. This led to the development of political machines, boss politics, and the spread of socialism. Exploitation of new immigrants by people in power kept many in poverty. The Padrone System was used against Greeks, Italians, Chinese, Japanese, and Mexicans. A family in the homeland would contract or sell their sons into servitude to a padrone. The terms of the contract ranged from a sum paid to the parents, to the passage for the child-worker. The indentured boy would then work for the padrone as agreed. The shoe shine market in Grand Rapids was a notorious exploiter of padrone system boys.[38] Industrialists added to the woes of immigrants by promoting divisions between ethnic groups. In the workplace, immigrants labored at repetitive, boring, and dangerous jobs. The evils brought on by industrialization and urbanization encouraged some of the new immigrants to support the Progressive movement of the early twentieth century.[39]

Eastern and southern European immigrants challenged the dominance of English and western European culture. They reshaped the evolution of diets, music, literature, language, and ideology in Michigan. Growing numbers of Catholics questioned Protestant influence, which led to greater religious diversity throughout the state.[40] The Eastern Orthodox Church grew as more Orthodox Christians entered Michigan. An active Jewish community made sure that Judaism had a prominent place in the religious life of Michigan. In 1919 Muslims built the first mosque in the United States in Highland Park.

The First World War and its aftermath exacerbated underlying social tensions. The war brought pressure on the people of German and Axis origins to shed their linguistic and cultural distinctiveness. By 1920, unemployed workers charged that the new immigrants and their alien ways were the cause of economic stagnation. Native-born citizens turned to the Americanization movement and promoted a melting-pot ideology, which encouraged people to give up their ethnic ways in favor of a more homogenous "American" identity.

In the 1920s, a wave of anticommunism that focused on immigrants who sympathized with unions unleashed the "Red Scare." The Ku Klux Klan burned crosses, ran a slate of political candidates, and "marched through Michigan streets proclaiming 100 percent Americanism." The brunt of their hatred fell upon immigrants, nonwhites, Catholics, and Jews. Even Henry Ford blamed the world's political and social ills on "the Jewish racial problem." Resentment against Canadians led to the Alien Registration Act of 1931 (later declared unconstitutional), and a repatriation program was set up to deport thousands of Mexicans in 1932.[41]

The ethnic portrait of Michigan in 1930 comprised a large number of groups who had come in the last thirty or forty years. Italians and Russians outnumbered the Dutch, Swedes, and Irish. Many emigrated from Albania, Czechoslovakia, Hungary, Yugoslavia, Romania, Greece, Russia, and Mexico. Armenians, Chaldeans, Macedonians, and Arabs added to the mix. By 1973 Detroit hosted the largest Macedonian and Arabic-speaking communities in North America. The Poles, however, became Michigan's most prominent "new" ethnic group of the twentieth century, and were second in number only to the Canadians.[42] Native Americans and African Americans remained distinct categories. As time passed, people of western European origins "melted" into a pattern of symbolic ethnicity, where they claimed to identify with a group without a commitment to the group's culture.[43]

### Modern Process

Before 1965, United States immigration policy favored western and northern Europeans. Four developments, however, brought profound changes to Michigan's culture and population: the influx of refugees, the Civil Rights movement, the 1965 United States Immigration Law, and illegal immigration.

As the Soviet Union dropped the Iron Curtain over eastern Europe, many refugees from occupied countries escaped to West Germany and from there entered the United States, including Michigan. Helped by churches and religious agencies, many people settled and started new lives in Michigan and established their old-world culture in their new land. Kalamazoo became the cultural center for Latvians, and Grass Lake became the cultural center for Romanians. Ethnic studies developed at Wayne State University, Western Michigan University, and the University of Michigan. These new entrants strongly supported

## REFUGEES FROM EUROPE 1945–1979

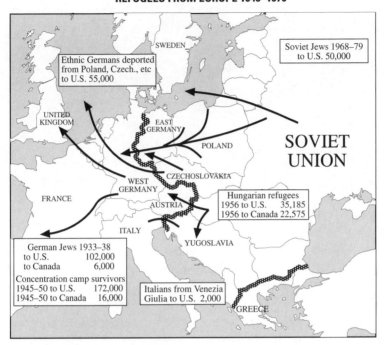

*After a large number of Jews fled Germany in 1933, refugees became a separate issue in American and Canadian immigration policy. The above map shows refugee movement from Europe to the United States and Canada. Adapted from John H. Long, "The Half-Open Door: Refugees from Hot and Cold Wars," in* The Settling of North America: The Atlas of the Great Migrations into North America from the Ice Age to the Present, *ed. Helen Hornbeck Tanner (New York: Macmillan, 1995), 148–49.*

American policies of containing communism while maintaining close ties with people back home.

Even for eastern European political refugees, coming to America did not bring complete freedom from the governments they had fled. The secret police had informers operating in the immigrant community, and if reprisals could not be performed in America, relatives in the homeland often suffered.

The Civil Rights movement heightened ethnic awareness and caused people to look into other areas of discriminatory behavior. This resulted

**IMMIGRANTS TO THE UNITIED STATES 1963–83**

CANADA
412,603

WEST GERMANY
272,521

SOVIET UNION
75,000 Jews

GREAT BRITAIN
369,004

POLAND
121,821

HUNGARY
29,445

IRELAND
57,427

YUGOSLAVIA
90,317

S. KOREA
341,416

PORTUGAL
192,940

ISRAEL
93,051

JAPAN
88,651

MEXICO
1, 181,760

CUBA
544,241

ITALY
92,254

HONG KONG
77,137

TAIWAN
325,025

HAITI
102,925

GUATEMALA
48,930

EL SALVADOR
57,565

DOMINICAN
REPUBLIC
260,000

EGYPT
46,050

INDIA
226,582

PHILIPPINES
505,582

NICARAGUA
25,877

COSTA RICA
29,158

COLUMBIA
158,218

BRAZIL
35,767

VIET NAM
300,000

PANAMA
45,552

PERU
52,246

AUSTRALIA
25,388

ARGENTINA
69,499

*This map identifies the countries that supplied the largest number of immigrants between 1963 and 1983. Adapted from Martin Gilbert,* The Dent Atlas of American History *(London: J. M. Dent), 115.*

in the scrutiny of immigration laws and led to changes in United States immigration policy. New policies enabled a new category of immigrant—the highly educated Asian professional—to come to Michigan. The NRI or Non-Resident Indian is a classification assigned to people whose origins are in India but who are living, or have lived, abroad and who identify themselves as a member of India's overseas community.

The 1965 Immigration Law eliminated the national origins clause, and, in essence, put all applicants on a equal basis for admission according to their qualifications and the needs of the United States. There was a ready pool of educated and qualified Asians and others to take advantage of the new regulations. As a result, Michigan, like the rest of the United States, received some of the best talent the world had to offer. People trained in countries such as the Philippines, India, and Venezuela filled voids in the medical, scientific, and engineering fields. They entered the middle and upper levels of Michigan society and resided in established neighborhoods alongside of old-stock Americans. They dressed and acted like their professional contemporaries. Having received a western education, they were acquainted with American ways and the English language.

On the surface, these people and their families seem assimilated. In reality, they compartmentalize their lives by being American outside their homes and maintaining traditional culture within their homes and ethnic communities. They work extremely hard to be proficient in their chosen careers. During the day and on the job, both men and women dress the same as their American-born colleagues and speak sophisticated English, sometimes with an accent. At home they enjoy traditional meals and music and communicate directly with folks back home over the telephone, by e-mail, or by exchanging videos. On weekends and holidays they often participate in festivities with other members of their ethnic group.

Few immigrants of today leave the old world behind. They send money back to family and friends. Some remain involved in the local and national issues of their homeland, others become government advisors, run for political office, or direct the administration of family assets in the homeland. They may form international networks that operate like multinational corporations with one brother in Hong Kong, another in Sydney, Australia and the third in Grand Rapids. They communicate by weekly phone calls and e-mail and shift assets with electronic rapidity.

All first generation immigrants have the overwhelming desire to be perceived as successful by family and friends back home. Frequently, the first pictures sent home are of the immigrants standing beside a new car. They send money home with glowing reports of success in America. The famed "American Letters" continue to the present day, but now the telephone enables people to speak directly in their native language with the family. In essence, the immigrant of today has not left one country for another, but has opted to become part of two societies, with the initial intention of using America as a base to become successful in the other. It is not common for the immigrant to remain in America, but to talk about "returning next year" or "returning after enough money is made." Since an integral part of the immigration experience today is the close connection between people living in Michigan and their countries of origin, any study of new immigrants must take into account the state of affairs in their homelands and the world.[44]

Large numbers of illegal immigrants and refugees from Cuba, South America, and Central America have fled to the United States in the last twenty years. Not as many have come to Michigan as have gone to California, Florida, New York, and some southern states. Illegal immigrants work on farms and in unskilled positions in urban areas. They are exploited, paid below minimum wage, and are tense with the fear of deportation. Their willingness to work for low wages enables employers to sell their products at lower prices and increased profits. Refugees who have come from war-torn El Salvador, Vietnam, and Laos often suffer from traumatic experiences, which saw them lose their homes and loved ones. Churches and social welfare agencies have provided counseling and have helped to settle many in Michigan.

Tensions within the new ethnic groups tend to increase as they grow, and their identity undergoes redefinition. When South Asians first came to Michigan, a person felt affinity to another South Asian, whether he or she came from India and Pakistan or was Hindu or Muslim. As the community grew, not only did Indians and Pakistanis have their own associations and see themselves as distinct communities, but within the Indian community, Bengalis, Gujaratis, and Punjabis perceived of themselves as separate groups.

In 1941 the contributors to *Michigan: A Guide to the Wolverine State* wrestled with the concept of Michigan's identity.[45] The writers focused on the production of copper, lumber, and automobiles, but did not dwell on the people. Michigan's identity is not in the manufacture of goods; it lies in the men, women, and children who have lived in the state. Michigan's people of diversity, representing many cultural heritages, have shaped the state's identity, meaning, and purpose in the past and will continue to do so in the future.

# Notes

## Issues in Ethnicity

1. Alejandro Portes and Reuben G. Rumbaut, *Immigrant America: A Portrait,* 2d ed. (Berkeley: University of California Press, 1996).
2. Reed Ueda, *Postwar Immigrant American: A Social History* (Boston: Bedford Books, 1994), 1.
3. James Axtell, *The Invasion Within: The Contest of Cultures in Colonial North America* (Oxford: Oxford University Press, 1985).
4. Manning Nash, *The Cauldron of Ethnicity in the Modern World* (Chicago: University of Chicago Press, 1989).
5. Joshua Fishman, *Language Loyalty in the United States* (London: Mouton, 1966), 43.
6. Joshua Fishman et al., *The Rise and Fall of the Ethnic Revival: Perspectives on Language and Ethnicity* (Berlin: Mouton, 1985), 172.
7. Richard Alba, *Ethnic Identity: The Transformation of White America* (New Haven: Yale University Press, 1990), 100.
8. Ibid.
9. Jack Glazier, "Secondary Migration and the Industrial Removal Office: The Politics of Jewish Immigrant Dispersion in the United States," in *Social Change and Applied Anthropology: Essays in Honor of David Brokensha,* ed. Miriam S. Chaiken and Anne K. Fleuret (Boulder, Colo.: Westview Press,

1990), 118–31; Jack Glazier, "Stigma, Identity and Sephardic-Ashkenazic Relations in Indianapolis," in *Persistence and Flexibility: Anthropological Perspectives on the American Jewish Experience,* ed. Walter P. Zener (Albany: State University of New York Press, 1988), 43–62.

10. Alba, *Ethnic Identity*; Herbert Gans, "Symbolic Ethnicity: The Future of Ethnic Groups and Cultures in America," *Ethnic and Racial Studies* 2, no. 1: 1–19; and Stephen Steinberg, *The Ethnic Myth* (Boston: Beacon Press, 1981).

11. Gans, "Symbolic Ethnicity," 9.

12. Laura Taxel, "Ethnic Eats: The Flavor of Cleveland," *Avenues* (May 1993): 22.

13. Alice Kehoe, *The Ghost Dance: Ethnohistory and Revitalization* (New York: Holt, Rinehart, and Winston, 1989), 76–77.

14. James Clifton, *The Invented Indian* (New Brunswick: Transaction Books, 1990), 32–33.

15. James Clifton, ed. *Being and Becoming Indian: Biographical Studies of North American Frontiers* (Chicago: Dorsey Press, 1989), 16.

16. *Statistical Abstract of the United States* (Washington, D.C.: U.S. Bureau of the Census, 1997), 18.

17. "Census Finds Many Claiming New Identity: Indian," *New York Times,* 5 March 1991, sec. A, pp. 1, 10.

18. "Hyphenated Americans," *Cleveland Plain Dealer,* 3 March 1991, sec. G, p. 1.

19. Bernard Wong, *Chinatown: Economic Adaptation and Ethnic Identity of the Chinese* (New York: Holt, Rinehart and Winston), 91.

20. Ibid., 79, 80.

21. Robert A. Rockaway, *The Jews of Detroit* (Detroit: Wayne State University Press, 1986), 140.

22. Irving Howe, *World of Our Fathers* (New York: Simon and Schuster, 1976), 253.

23. Alejandro Portes and Alex Stepick, *City on the Edge: The Transformation of Miami* (Berkeley: University of California Press, 1993).

## Ethnicity in Michigan

1. Traditions or mythology refers to how people perceive of themselves, which may or may not be true. The idea of Americans seeing themselves as rugged individuals in the tradition of the cowboy is an example.

2.  Culture, as used here is an abstract symbolic system composed of values, meanings and beliefs. See A. L. Kroeber and T. Parsons, "The Concepts of Cultural and Social Systems," *American Sociological Review* (1958): 582–83, and David M. Schneider, *American Kinship: A Cultural Account* (Englewood Cliffs: Prentice Hall, 1968).

3.  For a further elaboration of these concepts, see Arthur W. Helweg, "Comparing United States and Romanian Ethnic Dynamics: A Structural/ Symbolic Analysis" *Journal of Ethno Development* 3, no. 3 (1994): 66–76, and Arthur W. Helweg, "Punjabi Identity: A Structural/Symbolic Analysis," *Globalization and the Region: Explorations in Punjabi Identity*, ed. Pritam Singh and Shinder S. Thandi (Coventry: Association for Punjab Studies (U.K.), 1996).

4.  I use the term "process" and "classification" because we are examining a set of social dynamics where there is overlap in the process taking place. The concern here is not the time period nor trying to develop an evolutionary perspective. In fact, time-wise, overlap of these social processes is common.

5.  As one reads the rest of this essay, I would encourage frequent references to Appendices A and B which provide a quick overview of the peopling of Michigan.

6.  James A. Clifton, "The Potawatomi," in *People of the Three Fires*," ed. James A. Clifton, George L. Cornell, and James M. McClurken (Grand Rapids: Grand Rapids Intertribal Council, 1985), 45.

7.  See Henry R. Schoolcraft, *The Hiawatha Legends* (Au Train, Mich: Avery Color Studios, 1984) for an account of Native American interaction with the supernatural.

8.  See Charles E. Cleland, *Rites of Conquest: The History and Culture of Michigan's Native Americans* (Ann Arbor: University of Michigan Press, 1992); Bruce G. Trigger, ed., *Handbook of North American Indians, Northeast*, vol. 15 (Washington, D.C.: Smithsonian Institute, 1978); and George Cornell, "Unconquered Nations: The Native Peoples of Michigan," *Michigan Visions of Our Past*, ed. Richard J. Hathaway (East Lansing: Michigan State University Press, 1989).

9.  Cleland, *Rites of Conquest*, 59–61.

10. Sahlins classifies three types of reciprocity: generalized, balanced, and negative. Generalized reciprocity indicates a close relationship where a prestation is given without expecting a counter; nor do the participants

keep track of who has given what to whom. Balanced reciprocity is usually among equals and the participants are not so close and keep track. Negative reciprocity is when the participants try to maximize their assets from each other; there is no obligation closeness to this relationship. See Marshall D. Sahlins, "On the Sociology of Primitive Exchange," *The Relevance of Models for Social Anthropology, A.S.A. Monograph 1*, ed. Michael Banton (London: Tavistock Publications, 1965), 147.

11. For the Native Americans in Michigan, bands were groups of families that were all relatives. Clans were a group of bands, whose members claimed a common ancestor, whether or not it could actually be traced. The clan, however, had a totem. Clans that felt an affinity for each other were phratries. Tribes were seldom present because a chief was needed for a tribe and Michigan's Native Americans were egalitarian. See Cleland, *Rites of Conquest*, 39–54.

12. James A. Clifton, *Being and Becoming Indian: Biographical Sketches of the North American Frontier* (Chicago: The Dorsey Press, 1989).

13. See Andrew R. L. Cayton and Peter S. Onuf, *The Midwest and the Nation. Rethinking the History of an American Region* (Bloomington: Indiana University Press, 1990).

14. For further information, see Joe Grimm, comp. and ed., *Michigan Voices: Our State's History in the Words of the People Who Lived It* (Detroit: Detroit Free Press and Wayne State University Press, 1987), 27–48; Irving Rabideau, "French Canadians," in *The Peoples of Michigan*, vol. 2, ed. James M. Anderson and Iva A. Smith (Detroit: Ethnos Press, (1983); Lawrence M. Sommers, *Atlas of Michigan* (East Lansing: Michigan State University Press, 1977), 121; and Willis F. Dunbar, *Michigan: A History of the Wolverine State*, rev. ed. George S. May (Grand Rapids, Mich.: William B. Eerdmans Publishing Co., 1980), 200–1. In 1850 the highest number of immigrants came from New York, followed by Ohio, Vermont, Pennsylvania, Massachusetts, Connecticut, and New Jersey. "Old-Stock Americans" is a term that refers to people who came from New England and New York; see John G. Rice, "Old-Stock American," *They Chose Minnesota*, ed. June Drenning Holmquest (St. Paul: Minnesota Historical Society, 1981), 55–72. "Yankee" is a derivative of "Jan" and "Kaas," two Dutch words meaning "John Cheese." It was a derogatory term the Dutch used in referring to New Englanders; see Barbara Bilge, "Yankees," *The Peoples of Michigan*, vol. 2, 279.

15. U. P. Hendrick, *The Land of the Crooked Tree* (Detroit: Wayne State University Press, 1948), 10.

16. See Alexis de Tocqueville, "A Fortnight in the Wilderness," in *The Making of Michigan, 1820–1860*, ed. Justin L. Kestenbaum (Detroit: Wayne State University Press, 1990).

17. Bilge, "Yankees," 279.

18. Log cabins were not that numerous, for one of the first structures built by a community was a saw mill to cut timber, which supplied material for home construction. For Greek revival architecture, see Eric Freedman, *Pioneering Michigan* (Franklin, Mich.: Altwerger and Mandel Publishing Company, 1992), 254; and Willis F. Dunbar, *Michigan: A History of the Wolverine State*, 3rd rev. ed. George S. May (Grand Rapids, Mich.: William B. Eerdmans Publishing Co., 1995), 202.

19. Freedman, *Pioneering*, 49; Kestenbaum, *Making of Michigan*, Sylvia Prager et al., *Glimpses of the Past: Stories and Pictures of North Berrien Pioneer Families* (Coloma, Mich.: North Berrien Historical Society, 1992); Walter Romig, *Michigan Place Names* (Detroit: Wayne State University Press, 1986).

20. Larry B. Massie, *Copper Trails and Iron Rails: More Voyages into Michigan's Past* (Au Train, Mich.: Avery Color Studios, 1989), 220–23.

21. As quoted in Kestenbaum, *Making of Michigan*, 310.

22. Larry B. Massie, "Potawatomi Tears," in *Potawatomi Tears and Petticoat Pioneers* (Allegan Forest, Mich.: Prescilla Press, 1992), 13–35.

23. Leonard Dinnerstein and David Reimers, *Ethnic Americans: A History of Immigration*, 3d ed. (New York: Harper & Row, 1988), 4.

24. Joseph Ruff, "The Joys and Sorrows of an Emigrant Family," *Michigan History Magazine* 4, no. 1 (1920): 530–74.

25. Jeremy Kilar, *Michigan's Lumbertowns: Lumberman and Laborers in Saginaw, Bay City and Muskegon, 1870–1905* (Detroit: Wayne State University Press, 1990), 98–99, 177.

26. Dunbar, *Michigan*, rev. ed., 421–26. For more on lumbering see Theodore J. Karamkanski, *Deep Woods Frontier: A History of Logging in Northern Michigan* (Detroit: Wayne State University Press, 1989). For more information on mining see: Lew Allen Chase, "Michigan Copper Mines," *Michigan History* 29, no. 4 (1945): 479–88; J. E. Jopling, "Cornish Mines of the Upper Peninsula," *Michigan History* 12, no. 3 (1927): 554–67; Larry Lankton, *Cradle to Grave: Life, Work, and Death at the Lake Superior Copper Mines* (New

York: Oxford University Press, 1991); and Anthony S. Wax, "Calumet and Hecla Copper Mines: An Episode in the Economic Development of Michigan," *Michigan History* 16, no. 1 (1932): 5–41.

27. Susan Newhof Pyle, *A Most Superior Land: Life in the Upper Peninsula of Michigan* (Lansing, Mich.: Two Peninsula Press, 1983), 19.

28. George Erickson of Sweden described life in the Upper Peninsula in 1909. Excerpts from his letter provide a good example of an "American Letter":

> Here in America you don't have to go without work if you want something. I never had to look for work. I got it anyway, So there is certainly a difference between here and Sweden, where you have to bow and be humble and ask everywhere and still don't get any work anyway.
>
> I have it quite good here . . . I have the highest position in the company. If you aren't born here you can't get in with folks the way you would like.
>
> You know that those who are born here believe they are better than those who come from another country. . . .
>
> There probably isn't a country in the world that has as much graft as America. . . .
>
> You can imagine how hard it was to leave again but I also thought it was good to get away from all oppression and all that I would have to do if I stayed in Sweden. Here you are, in any event, a free man in a free country.

Taken from Grimm, *Voices*, 106–07.

29. Pyle, *Superior Land*, 19–23.

30. See Arthur W. Helweg, "Great Northern Migration," in *Encyclopedia of North American History*, consult. ed. John C. Super (New York: Marshall Cavendish Corp, 1999); and John H. Long, "People on the Move," in *The Settling of North America: The Atlas of the Great Migrations into North America from the Ice Age to the Present*, ed. Helen Hornbeck Tanner (New York: Macmillan, 1995), 149.

31. Dunbar, *Michigan*, rev. ed., 592–93; Grimm, *Michigan Voices*, 140.

32. Dunbar, *Michigan*, rev. ed., 390–92.

33. John Kern, *A Short History of Michigan* (Lansing: Michigan History Division, Michigan Department of State, 1977), 59.

34. See Leonard Dinnerstein and David M. Reimers, *Ethnic Americans: A History of Immigration and Assimilation* (New York: New York University Press, 1977), 36–55, for a thorough description of the composition and social behavior of new immigrants to America.

35. Dunbar, *Michigan*, rev. ed., 592–93.

36. Bryan Thompson, "Detroit Area Ethnic Groups 1988," a map prepared by the Urban Planning Department (Detroit: Wayne State University, 1989).

37. Sommers, *Atlas of Michigan*, 78.

38. Roger Daniels, *Coming to America: A History of Immigration and Ethnicity in American Life* (New York: HarperCollins, 1990), 996.

39. Senator Robert M. La Follette of Wisconsin led the Progressive opposition to the entrenched conservatism of the Republican Party. This lead to the formation of the Progressive Party in 1912.

40. Jeremy W. Kilar, "From Forest and Field to Factory: Michigan Workers and the Labor Movement," in *Michigan: Visions of Our Past*, 246–52.

41. Nora Fields, "Transitions and Turmoil: Social and Political Development in Michigan," in *Michigan: Visions of Our Past*, 205.

42. Dunbar, 3d rev. ed., 151–57.

43. See Richard D. Alba, *Ethnic Identity: The Transformation of White America* (New Haven: Yale University Press, 1990); and Herbert Gans, "Symbolic Ethnicity: The Future of Cultures in America," *Ethnic and Racial Studies* 2 (January 1979): 1–20.

44. See Arthur W. Helweg, *Sikhs in England*, 2d ed. (Delhi: Oxford University Press, 1986); Arthur W. Helweg and Usha M. Helweg, *An Immigrant Success Story: East Indians in America* (Philadelphia: University of Pennsylvania Press, 1990); Nina Glick Schiller, ed., *Towards a Transnational Perspective on Immigration: Race, Class and Nationalism Reconsidered* (New York: New York Academy of Sciences, 1992).

45. Writers' Program (Mich.), *Michigan: A Guide to the Wolverine State* (New York: Oxford University Press, 1941), 3–12.

# For Further Reference

Alba, Richard. *Ethnic Identity: The Transformation of White America*. New Haven, Conn.: Yale University Press, 1990.

Allen, James Paul, and Eugene James Turner. *We the People: An Atlas of America's Diversity*. New York: Macmillan, 1988.

Anderson, James, and Iva A. Smith. *Ethnic Groups in Michigan*. Detroit: Ethnos Press, 1983.

Axtell, James. *The Invasion Within: The Contest of Cultures in Colonial North America*. New York: Oxford University Press, 1985.

Barkan, Elliott Robert. *A Nation of Peoples: A Sourcebook on America's Multicultural Heritage*. Westport, Conn.: Greenwood Press, 1999.

Cleland, Charles E. *Rites of Conquest: The History and Culture of Michigan's Native Americans*. Ann Arbor: University of Michigan Press, 1992.

Clifton, James A., ed. *Being and Becoming Indian: Biographical Sketches of the North American Frontier*. Chicago: The Dorsey Press, 1989.

———. *The Invented Indian*. New Brunswick, N.J.: Transaction Books, 1990.

Daniels, Roger. *Coming to America: A History of Immigration and Ethnicity in American Life*. New York: HarperCollins, 1990.

Dunbar, Willis F. *Michigan: A History of the Wolverine State*. Rev. ed. by George S. May. Grand Rapids, Mich.: William B. Eerdmans Publishing Co., 1995.

Fishman, Joshua. *Language Loyalty in the United States*. London: Mouton, 1966.

Fishman, Joshua, et al. *The Rise and Fall of the Ethnic Revival: Perspectives on Language and Ethnicity.* Berlin: Mouton, 1985.

Garza, Rodolfo O. de la, et. al. *Latino Voices: Mexican, Puerto Rican, and Cuban Perspectives on American Politics.* Boulder, Colo.: Westview Press, 1992.

Glazer, Nathan. *We are all Multiculturalists Now.* Cambridge: Harvard University Press, 1997.

Glazier, Jack. *Dispersing the Ghetto: The Relocation of Jewish Immigrants Across America.* Ithaca, N.Y.: Cornell University Press, 1998.

Gonzales, Juan L. Jr. *Racial and Ethnic Groups in America.* Dubuque: Kendall/Hunt Publishing Company, 1993.

Graff, George P. *The People of Michigan.* Lansing: Michigan Department of Education, State Library Services, 1974.

Hathaway, Richard J., ed. *Michigan Visions of Our Past.* East Lansing: Michigan State University Press, 1989.

Helweg, Arthur W., and Usha M. Helweg. *An Immigrant Success Story: East Indians in North America.* Philadelphia: University of Pennsylvania Press, 1990.

Higham, John. *Send These to Me: Immigrants in Urban America.* Rev. ed. Baltimore: The Johns Hopkins University Press, 1984.

Hollinger, David. *Postethnic America: Beyond Multiculturalism.* New York: Basic Books, 1995.

Holmquist, June Drenning. *They Chose Minnesota: A Survey of the State's Ethnic Groups.* St. Paul: Minnesota Historical Society Press, 1981.

Howe, Irving. *World of Our Fathers.* New York: Simon and Schuster, 1976.

Kehoe, Alice. *The Ghost Dance: Ethnohistory and Revitalization.* New York: Holt, Rinehart, and Winston, 1989.

Kestenbaum, Justin L., ed. *The Making of Michigan, 1820–1860.* Detroit: Wayne State University Press, 1990.

Kilar, Jeremy. *Michigan's Lumbertowns: Lumberman and Laborers in Saginaw, Bay City and Muskegon, 1870–1905.* Detroit: Wayne State University Press, 1990.

Massie, Larry B. *Potawatomi Tears and Petticoat Pioneers: More of the Romances of Michigan's Past.* Allegan Forest, Mich.: The Priscilla Press, 1992.

Miller, Wayne Charles. *The Handbook of American Minorities.* New York: New York University of Press, 1976.

Nash, Manning. *The Cauldron of Ethnicity in the Modern World.* Chicago: University of Chicago Press, 1989.

Portes, Alejandro, ed. *The New Second Generation.* New York: Russell Sage, 1996.

Portes, Alejandro, and Alex Stepick. *City on the Edge: The Transformation of Miami.* Berkeley: University of California Press, 1993.

Portes, Alejandro, and Reuben G. Rumbaut. *Immigrant America: A Portrait,* second edition. Berkeley: University of California Press, 1996.

Rockaway, Robert A. *The Jews of Detroit.* Detroit: Wayne State University Press, 1986.

Sanjek, Roger. *The Future of Us All: Race and Neighborhood Politics in New York City.* Ithaca, N.Y.: Cornell University Press, 1998.

Tanner, Helen Hornbeck, ed. *The Settling of North America: The Atlas of the Great Migrations into North America from the Ice Age to the Present.* New York: Macmillan, 1995.

Ueda, Reed. *Postwar Immigrant America: A Social History.* Boston: Bedford Books, 1994.

White, Sid, and S. E. Solberg, eds. *Peoples of Washington: Perspectives on Cultural Diversity.* Pullman: Washington State University Press, 1989.

Wong, Bernard. *Chinatown: Economic Adaptation and Ethnic Identity of the Chinese.* New York: Holt, Rinehart and Winston.

# Michigan Ethnic Group Table

*Jeffrey D. Bonevich*

The following table of ethnic groups is compiled from several sources (listed after the table). The purpose of this table is to provide the reader with a quick reference guide to the ethnic groups of Michigan. The table is naturally limited in the scope and depth of the information covered. In addition, any inaccuracies in the data presented here originates with the source and is compounded by editing to fit the space requirements of the table. Neither of these problems can be resolved here, and the reader is referred to the sources cited below for more detailed information on the groups listed.

## Ethnic Groups in the State of Michigan

### African Americans

ORIGIN: Western Africa (Canada, Southern U.S.)

ARRIVAL IN MICHIGAN: 1840–80s, 1940 to present (present as early as 1700)

OCCUPATIONS: Throughout Lower Peninsula, predominantly in Detroit: industrial, political, educational, professional, and public occupations

COMMENTS: Many descend from slaves from Africa, and white and Native American ancestors; major proponent in American civil rights movements; largest minority group in state

## Africans

ORIGIN: Cameroon, Ethiopia, Ghana, Liberia, Nigeria, Sierra Leone, Tanzania
ARRIVAL IN MICHIGAN: 1970–present
OCCUPATIONS: University students, professionals
COMMENTS: Often subsumed by African American organizations

## Albanians

ORIGIN: Yugoslavia (Kosova, Macedonia, Montenegro)
ARRIVAL IN MICHIGAN: 1945–60s
OCCUPATIONS: Detroit: food service
COMMENTS: Fled Communist takeover

## Amish

ORIGIN: Switzerland
ARRIVAL IN MICHIGAN: 1895 first settlement, 1910 earliest settlements existing
   today; 1970 major influx
OCCUPATIONS: Rural family farms in Lower Peninsula, crafts, bakeries, chickens,
   garden produce
COMMENTS: Maintain separateness from dominant society, limit use of modern
   technology, wear distinctive garb, no schooling beyond 8th grade, do not
   accept social security benefits, religion structures world view

## Arabic speakers

ORIGIN: Algeria, Bahrain, Egypt, Iraq, Jordan, Kuwait, Lebanon, Libya, Morocco,
   Palestine, Qatar, Saudi Arabia, Oman, Syria, Tunisia, United Arab Republic,
   Yemen (U.S.)
ARRIVAL IN MICHIGAN: 1880 to present
OCCUPATIONS: Detroit: auto industry, professionals, small business, food service
COMMENTS: Largest Arab urban population in U.S.; both Muslim and Christian
   sects (tend to settle along these lines); later immigration reflects post-WW II
   unrest in Middle East

## Armenians

ORIGIN: Turkey, Iran, Lebanon, Syria
ARRIVAL IN MICHIGAN: 1890–1920s, 1940s, 1980s to present
OCCUPATIONS: Detroit: blue collar, professionals, engineers, doctors, lawyers

COMMENTS: Strong Christian affiliations; maintain strong ties to homelands; fled turmoil in Lebanon, Iran, and Soviet Union

## Asian Indians
ORIGIN: India
ARRIVAL IN MICHIGAN: 1920s, 1970s to present
OCCUPATIONS: Detroit: doctors, scientists, engineers
COMMENTS: Came for education and employment opportunities

## Assyrians
ORIGIN: Iran, Iraq, Russia (U.S.)
ARRIVAL IN MICHIGAN: 1910–1920
OCCUPATIONS: Flint: farming and auto industry
COMMENTS: Assyrian American National Union of Flint

## Australians and New Zealanders
ORIGIN: Australia, New Zealand (U.S.)
ARRIVAL IN MICHIGAN: 19th century, 1940s
COMMENTS: Few in numbers; descendants of English, Scots, and Irish

## Austrians
ORIGIN: Austria (Canada)
ARRIVAL IN MICHIGAN: 1919–29, 1940s
OCCUPATIONS: Detroit: tool-and-die and auto industries, professionals
COMMENTS: Strong ties with Austria

## Bangladeshi
ORIGIN: Bangladesh
ARRIVAL IN MICHIGAN: 1970s to present
OCCUPATIONS: Professionals, doctors, engineers
COMMENTS: Came for educational and employment opportunities

## Belgians (or Flemish)
ORIGIN: Belgium
ARRIVAL IN MICHIGAN: 1830–60s, 1900–50s

OCCUPATIONS: Upper Peninsula: mining and lumbering; Detroit: brick-making, farming, small business, construction and auto industries

COMMENTS: Fled cultural oppression of Belgian government; maintain cultural exchange with Belgium; publish *Belgian Gazette*

## Bosnian Muslims

ORIGIN: Yugoslavia

ARRIVAL IN MICHIGAN: 1900, 1940s

OCCUPATIONS: Detroit

## Bulgarians

ORIGIN: Macedonia, Thrace

ARRIVAL IN MICHIGAN: 1910–40s

OCCUPATIONS: Detroit, Battle Creek: farmers, merchants, professional, and small business

COMMENTS: Largest population in U.S.; recent resurgence of interest in cultural heritage

## Byelorussians

ORIGIN: Byelorussia (U.S.)

ARRIVAL IN MICHIGAN: 1880–1920, 1940s

OCCUPATIONS: Grand Rapids: laborers and wood workers; Albion: iron mining; Saginaw: sugar beet farming; Detroit: industry, professionals

COMMENTS: Socially cohesive but culturally and politically diverse; active in seeking independence of Byelorussia from the Soviet Union

## Canadians (Anglophone)

ORIGIN: Canada

ARRIVAL IN MICHIGAN: 1860–90, 1930–60s

OCCUPATIONS: No concentrations: white collar and manufacturing labor, professionals, lawyers, doctors, business

COMMENTS: Form no cohesive social or cultural groups; majority have been incorporated into mainstream American society

## Caribbean Islanders

ORIGIN: Guyana, Belize, West Indies (U.S.)

ARRIVAL IN MICHIGAN: 1900–50s

OCCUPATIONS: Detroit: small and professional business, tailors, cleaners, auto and railway industries, students, politicians (Harold Lucas)

COMMENTS: Descendants of African slaves; prominent in early economic development in Detroit; involved in universal civil rights for blacks

## Carpatho-Rusyns

ORIGIN: Czechoslovakia, Poland, Hungary, Ukraine

ARRIVAL IN MICHIGAN: 1915–40s

OCCUPATIONS: Flint, Detroit: auto industry, professionals

COMMENTS: Undergoing incorporation into American culture, although interest in heritage is growing

## Chaldeans

ORIGIN: Iraq (many from a single village, Telkaif)

ARRIVAL IN MICHIGAN: 1900–12, 1960–70s

OCCUPATIONS: Detroit: grocery business, professionals, students

COMMENTS: Largest population in U.S.; all are Catholics

## Chinese

ORIGIN: China (U.S.)

ARRIVAL IN MICHIGAN: 1870 to present

OCCUPATIONS: Detroit: domestic service, small business, students, professionals; Upper Peninsula: mining

COMMENTS: Subject to intense labor discrimination until 1943; many have emigrated to other states in the U.S.

## Copts

ORIGIN: Egypt

OCCUPATIONS: Detroit: professionals, higher education

COMMENTS: Large portion emigrated to California

## Cornish

ORIGIN: Cornwall in England

ARRIVAL IN MICHIGAN: 1830–1920s

OCCUPATIONS: Upper Peninsula: copper and iron mining; Detroit: auto industry

COMMENTS: Left England during period of decline in mining; emigrated to Detroit following decline in mining in Upper Peninsula.

## Croatians

ORIGIN: Hungary

ARRIVAL IN MICHIGAN: 1882–1920s, 1940–50s

OCCUPATIONS: Calumet: lumbering, copper mining; Detroit: auto industry, business

COMMENTS: Largest population in U.S.; Croatian Board of Trade aides in developing business interests

## Czechs

ORIGIN: Czechoslovakia

ARRIVAL IN MICHIGAN: 1855–1920s, 1970s

OCCUPATIONS: Grand Traverse Region: farming; Detroit, Saginaw, Flint, Lansing: auto industry, craftspeople

COMMENTS: Many served during U.S. Civil War; Czech press has greatly influenced immigrant philosophy

## Danes

ORIGIN: Denmark

ARRIVAL IN MICHIGAN: 1860 to early 1900s

OCCUPATIONS: Detroit: tradespeople, craftspeople; West Michigan: farming, small business

COMMENTS: Danish Folk School in Newaygo County was early educational center; Greenville, summer Danish festival; incorporated into mainstream American culture

## Dutch

ORIGIN: Netherlands

ARRIVAL IN MICHIGAN: 1840–80s, 1940s

OCCUPATIONS: Holland, Grand Rapids, Muskegon: lumbering, farming, tanning, furniture, industry, fruit growers

COMMENTS: Instrumental in developing Southwest Michigan; Hope College and Calvin College began as Dutch schools

## English

ORIGIN: England

ARRIVAL IN MICHIGAN: 1815–90s, 1940s, 1960s

OCCUPATIONS: Detroit

COMMENTS: Some members of Shaker community

## Estonians

ORIGIN: Estonia

ARRIVAL IN MICHIGAN: 1920s, 1940s

OCCUPATIONS: Detroit, Ann Arbor, Grand Rapids, Saginaw

COMMENTS: Legion of Estonian Liberation is world-wide liberation organization

## Filipinos

ORIGIN: Philippine Islands

ARRIVAL IN MICHIGAN: after 1965

OCCUPATIONS: Professionals (medical), teachers

COMMENTS: Difficulty in gaining recognition for education and degrees from
   homeland

## Finns

ORIGIN: Finland

ARRIVAL IN MICHIGAN: 1864–80s

OCCUPATIONS: Upper Peninsula: copper mining, farming; Lower Peninsula: lumbering, farming; Detroit: auto industry

COMMENTS: Suomi College; active in early labor movements; large number of
   ethnic publications

## French Canadians

ORIGIN: France and Canada

ARRIVAL IN MICHIGAN: 1700–60, 1840–1910

OCCUPATIONS: Detroit; Saginaw, Bay City: lumbering, farming; Upper Peninsula:
   lumbering, mining, fur trading

COMMENTS: First European settlers in Michigan; followed logging industry into
   Michigan; established trade with Native Americans; subjected to British,
   then American control in late 1700s

## Frisians

ORIGIN: Netherlands, Germany

ARRIVAL IN MICHIGAN: 1840s

OCCUPATIONS: Holland and Grand Rapids: farming, industry

COMMENTS: Closely aligned with Dutch settlement of Michigan

## Germans

ORIGIN: Germany

ARRIVAL IN MICHIGAN: 1830–90s, 1920–30s

OCCUPATIONS: Detroit, Frankenmuth, Saginaw: farming, lumbering, brewing, auto industry, manufacturing

COMMENTS: Arrived in small religious groups initially; major industrial recruitment to settle in Michigan; support labor movements

## Greeks

ORIGIN: Greece (particularly the Dodecanese islands and Peloponnesus region), Asia Minor, Egypt, Cyprus, Black Sea region

ARRIVAL IN MICHIGAN: 1880s, 1910–40s, 1960–70s

OCCUPATIONS: Throughout Michigan: food service, small and professional business, skilled laborers

COMMENTS: Detroit's "Greektown" now business, not cultural center; American Hellenic Council, Greek-American Medical Association are Michigan based; friction between early and later immigrants is a problem

## Gypsies

ORIGIN: Hungary (originated in India in 1300s)

OCCUPATIONS: Detroit and Dearborn: entertainment (music)

## Hispanics and Latinos

ORIGIN: Mexico, Puerto Rico, Cuba, Central America, South American countries, Texas, Southwest U.S.)

ARRIVAL IN MICHIGAN: 1910–20, 1950–70s (seasonal migration)

OCCUPATIONS: Detroit, Pontiac, Flint: railway labor, auto industry, professionals; throughout Michigan: steel industry, farm labor

COMMENTS: Spanish and Mexicans hold Fort St. Joseph in 1781; gaining political presence through unified cultural efforts

## Hungarians (Magyars)

ORIGIN: Hungary, Romania, Austria, Yugolavia, Czechoslovakia, (U.S.)

ARRIVAL IN MICHIGAN: 1900–20s, 1950s to present

OCCUPATIONS: Detroit (Delray):, Flint (Burton) auto and other industries, retail and wholesale business, professionals

COMMENTS: Maintain ties with homeland, many Michigan-based cultural organizations; highly involved in musical and visual arts

## Icelanders

ORIGIN: Iceland

ARRIVAL IN MICHIGAN: 1940s

OCCUPATIONS: Detroit

## Indochinese

ORIGIN: Vietnam, Cambodia, Laos, Hmong

ARRIVAL IN MICHIGAN: 1970s

OCCUPATIONS: Detroit, Grand Rapids: underemployed.

COMMENTS: Refugees finding acceptance into U.S. difficult

## Iranians

ORIGIN: Iran

ARRIVAL IN MICHIGAN: 1960–70s

OCCUPATIONS: Detroit: doctors, technical professions, students

COMMENTS: Political turmoil in homelands led to discrimination in U.S.

## Irish

ORIGIN: Ireland (Scotland, Canada)

ARRIVAL IN MICHIGAN: 1820–1900s

OCCUPATIONS: Detroit: farming, railroad construction, labor, professionals, industry

COMMENTS: Many fled pre-1840 famines in Europe; highly incorporated into mainstream American culture yet maintain strong ethnic identity and cultural exchange groups

## Italians

ORIGIN: Italy

ARRIVAL IN MICHIGAN: 1870–1920s

OCCUPATIONS: Upper Peninsula: farming, mining; Detroit: industry, small business

COMMENTS: Participants in early French exploration and settlement; active in early labor movements

## Japanese

ORIGIN: Japan (West Coast of U.S.)

ARRIVAL IN MICHIGAN: 1940s

OCCUPATIONS: Detroit: professional; ten percent are Japanese businessmen temporarily in Detroit

COMMENTS: Fled anti-Japanese sentiments fed by WWII; some still practice Buddhism

## Jews

ORIGIN: Germany, Eastern Europe, U.S.S.R.

ARRIVAL IN MICHIGAN: German Jews 1840–80; Eastern Jews 1880 to present

OCCUPATIONS: Detroit: business, retail trade, professionals (doctors, lawyers, dentists, accountants, teachers, social workers, etc.)

COMMENTS: Some involved in early French and English exploration and settlement; many prominent political and cultural leaders have come from Detroit group

## Koreans

ORIGIN: Korea

ARRIVAL IN MICHIGAN: 1960–70s

OCCUPATIONS: Detroit: medical professionals and engineers

COMMENTS: Fled political upheaval in homeland; mostly from upper class Korean families

## Latvians

ORIGIN: Latvia

ARRIVAL IN MICHIGAN: 1940s

OCCUPATIONS: Southern Michigan

COMMENTS: Fled when U.S.S.R. invaded during WW II

## Lithuanians

ORIGIN: Lithuania

ARRIVAL IN MICHIGAN: 1860–1910s

OCCUPATIONS: Grand Rapids: furniture industry, lumbering, mining; Detroit

COMMENTS: Twenty percent of entire population fled tsarist oppression, with largest portion going to U.S.

## Macedonians

ORIGIN: Yugoslavia, Greece, Bulgaria

ARRIVAL IN MICHIGAN: 1920s, 1960–70s

OCCUPATIONS: Detroit: auto industry, food service; Kalamazoo, Battle Creek

COMMENTS: Culturally divided by early political struggles, but unifying due to Yugoslavian encouragement of national identity, in homeland and in U.S.

## Maltese

ORIGIN: Malta (Australia)

ARRIVAL IN MICHIGAN: 1890–1920s, 1940–50s

OCCUPATIONS: Detroit: auto industry

COMMENTS: Left crowded conditions; mostly incorporated into American culture, though some associations maintained

## Manx

ORIGIN: Isle of Man

ARRIVAL IN MICHIGAN: 1890s

OCCUPATIONS: Upper Peninsula: mining

## Montenegrins

ORIGIN: Yugoslavia

ARRIVAL IN MICHIGAN: late 1800s, early 1900s

OCCUPATIONS: Detroit: industry, small business

COMMENTS: Many returned home to aid in WW II, and many then returned to the U.S.

## Moroccans

ORIGIN: Morocco

ARRIVAL IN MICHIGAN: 1950s

OCCUPATIONS: Detroit: professionals
COMMENTS: Mostly of Jewish descent

### Muslims (includes Turks, Kurds)

ORIGIN: Turkey, Iraq, Iran, Syria
ARRIVAL IN MICHIGAN: 1900–14, 1940s
OCCUPATIONS: Detroit: auto industry, unskilled labor
COMMENTS: Mostly incorporated into American culture

### Native Americans *(mostly Ottawa, Potawatomi, and Ojibwa)*

ORIGIN: Native to Michigan, elsewhere in North America
ARRIVAL IN MICHIGAN: present for at least 11,000 years
OCCUPATIONS: Throughout state; concentrations in Detroit, Mt. Pleasant, and
    Upper Peninsula; more rural than other groups
COMMENTS: Long history of cultural, social, and biological change; modern
    "Indians" are an amalgam of peoples from Europe and other parts of the
    world, not solely native to Michigan

### Norwegians

ORIGIN: Norway
ARRIVAL IN MICHIGAN: 1830–1920s
OCCUPATIONS: Upper and Lower Peninsula: mining, lumbering; Detroit: auto
    industry
COMMENTS: Small population living in Detroit

### Pakistanis

ORIGIN: Pakistan
ARRIVAL IN MICHIGAN: 1970s
OCCUPATIONS: Urban areas in Lower Peninsula: professionals (medical), engineers

### Poles

ORIGIN: Poland (Eastern U.S.)
ARRIVAL IN MICHIGAN: 1880–1920s
OCCUPATIONS: Detroit, Hamtramck, Grand Rapids, Bay City, Saginaw, Flint: lum-
    bering, farming, industry
COMMENTS: Most households continued to speak Polish as their only or main

language until at least 40 years ago; present in Detroit in late 1800s; largest immigrant population in Michigan

## Polynesians

ORIGIN: Hawaii, Samoa, New Zealand, Tahiti, etc.

OCCUPATIONS: Small in numbers

## Portuguese

ORIGIN: Portugal

OCCUPATIONS: Dearborn and Detroit

## Romanians

ORIGIN: Greater Romania and South-Eastern European countries

ARRIVAL IN MICHIGAN: 1920–30s

OCCUPATIONS: Concentrated in Detroit, Flint, and suburbs, but scattered throughout Michigan: auto industry, small business, education, medical, professional, engineers, constructions, and technicians

COMMENTS: Largest Romanian coummunity outside Romania and in all North America; spiritual center of the Romanian Orthodox Church in North and South America

## Russians

ORIGIN: U.S.S.R.

ARRIVAL IN MICHIGAN: 1910–20s, 1940s

OCCUPATIONS: Detroit

COMMENTS: Russian Balalaika Orchestra of Detroit

## San Marinese

ORIGIN: San Marino

ARRIVAL IN MICHIGAN: early 1900s

OCCUPATIONS: Detroit: factory and residential construction

## Scots and Scotch-Irish

ORIGIN: Scotland (Ireland, U.S.)

ARRIVAL IN MICHIGAN: mid- to late-1800s

OCCUPATIONS: Saginaw Bay area: farming; Detroit

## Serbians

ORIGIN: Yugoslavia

ARRIVAL IN MICHIGAN: 1898–1910s, 1940s, 1960s

OCCUPATIONS: Detroit: industry, small business

COMMENTS: Many returned home to fight during WW I before U.S. involvement

## Slovaks

ORIGIN: Czechoslovakia (U.S.)

ARRIVAL IN MICHIGAN: 1880–1940s

OCCUPATIONS: Upper Peninsula.: mining; Saginaw: farming; Detroit: auto industry

## Slovenes

ORIGIN: Yugoslavia (U.S.)

ARRIVAL IN MICHIGAN: 1896–1910s, 1920s

OCCUPATIONS: Upper Peninsula: mining; Detroit: auto industry

COMMENTS: Bishop Baraga instructed and converted many Native Americans in 1830s

## Swedes

ORIGIN: Sweden

ARRIVAL IN MICHIGAN: 1850–90s, 1920s

OCCUPATIONS: Western Michigan: lumbering, railroads; Upper Peninsula: mining; Detroit: auto industry, engineering, professional

COMMENTS: Active church and organizational life: Detroit-Swedish Council, Swedish Club, Jenny Lind Society, SWEA, Swedish Womens Club, singing groups

## Swiss

ORIGIN: Switzerland

ARRIVAL IN MICHIGAN: mid-1800s

OCCUPATIONS: Detroit: farming, professional

COMMENTS: Detroit Swiss Society

## Thais

ORIGIN: Thailand

ARRIVAL IN MICHIGAN: 1960–70s

COMMENTS: Small in numbers

## Turks

ORIGIN: Turkey

ARRIVAL IN MICHIGAN: 1903–20s, 1940s

OCCUPATIONS: Detroit: auto industry

COMMENTS: Initially Ottoman Muslim identity, later Turkish national, with differences arising between Turks and Kurds tied to events in Turkey; Kizil Ay (Muslim Red Cross)

## Ukrainians

ORIGIN: Ukraine

ARRIVAL IN MICHIGAN: 1885–1920s; 1940s

OCCUPATIONS: Lansing, Saginaw, Grand Rapids: farming; Detroit, Flint: auto industry, professional

COMMENTS: Some forced from home country following forced service in German Army in WW II; many Ukrainian cultural centers in Detroit area

## Volga and Volhynia-Germans

ORIGIN: Eastern Russia (Germans expatriated to Russia in Eighteenth Century)

ARRIVAL IN MICHIGAN: 1890–10

OCCUPATIONS: Saginaw and Berrien counties, Sebewaing: farming, fruit and nursery farming, craftsmen

COMMENTS: Brought sugar beet industry to Michigan; settled in small community groups

## Welsh

ORIGIN: Wales (Eastern U.S.)

ARRIVAL IN MICHIGAN: late 1800s to early 1900s

OCCUPATIONS: Upper Peninsula: mining; Detroit

COMMENTS: Detroit Welsh Society; mostly incorporated into American culture

## Sources

1. Anderson, James, and Iva A. Smith. *Ethnic Groups in Michigan.* Detroit: Ethnos Press, 1983.

2. Graff, George P. *The People of Michigan.* Lansing: Michigan Department of Education, State Library Servies, 1974.

3. Helweg, Arthur W., ed. *Ethnic Michigan.* Unpublished ms.

# Timeline Charts

*Jeffrey D. Bonevich*

The timeline for immigration into Michigan is broken into two major periods. The first chart covers ethnic groups that arrived in Michigan during the pre-industrial period of Michigan history from the arrival of the ancestors of the Native Americans around 10,000 years ago to the beginning of the twentieth century. The second chart covers immigration during the industrial and postindustrial periods from the development of Detroit-area industry until the present. The dashed line demarcates the (major) period of immigration for the ethnic group(s) indicated. As will be noted, some groups arrived during both time periods. In addition, ethnic groups have been grouped together by their economic pursuits. For example, on Chart 1, Indians and French Canadians participated in the fur trade, while Germans, Norwegians, Swedes, and Lithuanians participated primarily in lumbering. The data for these charts were obtained from Appendix A, the table on ethnic groups in Michigan. As with the table, these charts are to provide a quick historical reference to immigration into Michigan, they are not meant to be definitive.

**CHART 1. Major Periods of Immigration for Michigan, 8000 B.C. to 1900**

| PREHISTORY | FRONTIER AND SETTLEMENT |
|---|---|

Fur Trade

Commercial Lumbering

Agriculture

Mining

Native Americans

French Canadians

Germans, Norwegians

Swedes

Lithuanians

8000 B.C. | A.D. 1600 | 1700 | 1800 | 1820 | 1850 | 1860 | 1870 | 1880 | 1890

Irish, Scots, Scotch-Irish, English
Belgians
African Americans, Dutch, Frisians, Swiss
Jews
Danes
British Canadians
Volga and Volhynia Germans
Cornish
Finns
Italians, Chinese
Croatians
Welsh, Manx

**CHART 2. Major Periods of Immigration for Michigan, 1880–1990**

| ECONOMIC DEVELOPMENT AND THE INDUSTRIAL AGE | POST-WAR DEPRESSION | POST-INDUSTRIALISM |
|---|---|---|

Columns: 1880 | 1890 | 1900 | 1910 | 1920 | 1930 | 1940 | 1950 | 1960 | 1970 | 1980

Old Automobile Industry

Other Industry

Small Business

Business and Professional

Auto Industry

Slovaks

Cornish, Norwegians

Czechs

Ukranians, Croatians, Maltese

Arabs

Muslims (Turks, Kurds, and Bosnian Muslims)

Belgians

Hungarians, Slovenes

Hispanics

Assyrians

Carpatho-Rusyns

Romanians, Germans

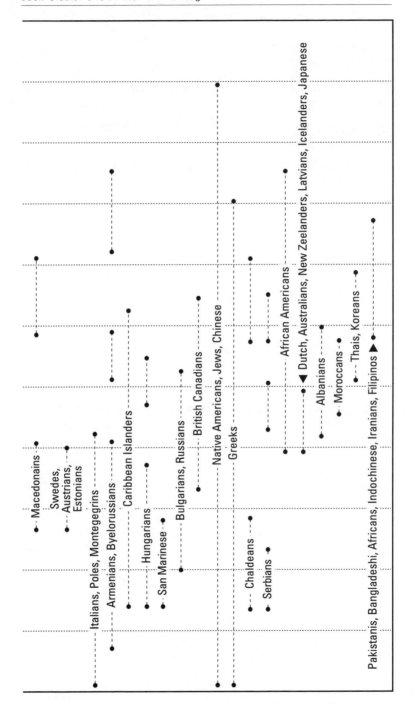

## Sources

1. Anderson, James, and Iva A. Smith. *Ethnic Groups in Michigan.* Detroit: Ethnos Press, 1983.

2. Graff, George P. *The People of Michigan.* Lansing: Michigan Department of Education, State Library Servies, 1974.

3. Helweg, Arthur W., ed. *Ethnic Michigan.* Unpublished ms.

Appendix C

# Michigan Foreign Born

This table, showing the foreign-born population, helps to analyze the immigrant population in Michigan. This results in a better understanding of the foreign population dynamics as they relate to Michigan.

| | 1860 | 1870 | 1880 | 1890 | 1900 | 1910 | 1920 | 1930 | 1940 | 1950 | 1960 | 1970 | 1980 | 1990 |
|---|---|---|---|---|---|---|---|---|---|---|---|---|---|---|
| SOUTH AMERICA | | | | | | | | | | | | | 5,553 | 5,367 |
| Argentina | | | | | | | | | | | | | | 1,113 |
| Bolivia | | | | | | | | | | | | | | 186 |
| Brazil | | | | | | | | | | | | | | 1,011 |
| Chile | | | | | | | | | | | | | | 374 |
| Columbia | | | | | | | | | | | | | | 935 |
| Equador | | | | | | | | | | | | | | 252 |
| Guyana | | | | | | | | | | | | | | 330 |
| Paraguay | | | | | | | | | | | | | | 104 |
| Peru | | | | | | | | | | | | | | 415 |
| Surinam | | | | | | | | | | | | | | 10 |
| Uruguay | | | | | | | | | | | | | | 123 |
| Venezuela | | | | | | | | | | | | | | 429 |
| Other South America | | | | | | | | | | | | | | 85 |
| AFRICA | | | | | | | | | | | | | 5,244 | 6,280 |
| Algeria | | | | | | | | | | | | | | 99 |
| Angola | | | | | | | | | | | | | | 9 |
| Cameroon | | | | | | | | | | | | | | 58 |
| Cape Verde | | | | | | | | | | | | | | 7 |
| Egypt | | | | | | | | | | | | | | 1,291 |
| Ethiopia | | | | | | | | | | | | | | 401 |
| Ghana | | | | | | | | | | | | | | 332 |
| Kenya | | | | | | | | | | | | | | 295 |
| Liberia | | | | | | | | | | | | | | 218 |
| Libya | | | | | | | | | | | | | | 121 |
| Morocco | | | | | | | | | | | | | | 179 |
| Nigeria | | | | | | | | | | | | | | 1,142 |

| | 1860 | 1870 | 1880 | 1890 | 1900 | 1910 | 1920 | 1930 | 1940 | 1950 | 1960 | 1970 | 1980 | 1990 |
|---|---|---|---|---|---|---|---|---|---|---|---|---|---|---|
| Senegal | | | | | | | | | | | | | | 43 |
| Sierra Leone | | | | | | | | | | | | | | 91 |
| Somalia | | | | | | | | | | | | | | 19 |
| South Africa | | | | | | | | | | | | | | 185 |
| Sudan | | | | | | | | | | | | | | 87 |
| Tanzania | | | | | | | | | | | | | | 131 |
| Tunisia | | | | | | | | | | | | | | 119 |
| Uganda | | | | | | | | | | | | | | 142 |
| Zaire | | | | | | | | | | | | | | 84 |
| Zambia | | | | | | | | | | | | | | 104 |
| Zimbabwe | | | | | | | | | | | | | | 124 |
| North Africa | | | | | | | | | | | | | 1,938 | |
| Other Africa | | | | | | | | | | | | | 3,306 | 698 |
| OCEANIA | | | | | | | | | | | | | | 1,211 |
| Australia | | | | | | | | | | | | | | 836 |
| Fiji | | | | | | | | | | | | | | 53 |
| Micronesia | | | | | | | | | | | | | | 31 |
| New Zealand | | | | | | | | | | | | | | 217 |
| Tongo | | | | | | | | | | | | | | 2 |
| Western Samoa | | | | | | | | | | | | | | 24 |
| Other Oceania | | | | | | | | | | | | | | 46 |
| EUROPE | | | | | | 198,211 | 145,052 | | | | | 7,881 | 198,211 | 145,052 |
| Albania | | | | | | | | | | | | | | 485 |
| Austria | 660 | 1,974 | 2,814 | 5,950 | 8,209 | 16,442 | 22,004 | 13,299 | 17,916 | 15,072 | | | 5,046 | 2,577 |
| Belgium | 597 | 8,332 | 970 | 2,232 | 2,647 | 5,683 | 10,501 | 13,931 | 5,441 | 10,518 | | | | 2,559 |
| Bulgaria | | | | | | | | | | | | | | 296 |
| Czech Republic | | | | | | | | | | | | 4,553 | | |

|  | 1860 | 1870 | 1880 | 1890 | 1900 | 1910 | 1920 | 1930 | 1940 | 1950 | 1960 | 1970 | 1980 | 1990 |
|---|---|---|---|---|---|---|---|---|---|---|---|---|---|---|
| Czechoslovakia | 192 | 1,354 | 3,513 | 6,335 | 6,390 | 6,313 | 11,151 | 17,646 | 12,725 | 12,168 |  | 6,871 | 4,368 | 2,867 |
| Denmark |  |  |  |  |  |  | 7,178 | 5,441 | 5,441 | 4,219 |  | 2,379 |  | 775 |
| Estonia |  |  |  |  |  |  |  |  |  |  | 2,801 |  |  | 180 |
| Finland |  |  |  |  |  |  |  | 27,022 | 21,151 | 15,503 |  |  |  | 1,110 |
| France | 2,466 | 3,121 | 3,203 | 5,182 | 2,590 | 2,418 | 4,171 | 4,581 | 3,366 | 3,632 | 7,702 | 3,120 | 3,051 | 2,361 |
| Germany | 38,177 | 64,147 | 89,085 | 135,508 | 125,074 | 105,912 | 86,047 | 81,714 | 59,783 | 45,632 | 58,942 | 34,537 | 30,544 | 24,135 |
| Greece |  |  |  | 10 | 134 | 1,195 | 7,115 | 10,061 | 8,989 |  | 16,022 | 7,760 | 7,808 | 5,787 |
| Hungary |  | 144 | 193 | 637 | 835 | 11,597 |  | 19,188 |  |  | 8,482 | 9,743 | 6,592 | 3,872 |
| Iceland |  |  |  |  |  |  |  |  |  |  |  |  |  | 80 |
| Ireland | 8,405 | 8,403 | 7,776 | 6,489 |  |  |  |  | 29,593 | 18,818 | 13,752 | 4,367 | 3,715 | 2,303 |
| Italy | 87 | 110 | 555 | 3,088 | 6,178 | 16,850 | 30,216 | 41,087 | 40,631 | 38,937 | 36,670 | 31,986 | 26,238 | 18,549 |
| Latvia |  |  |  |  |  |  | 1,517 | 8,403 | 8,403 | 7,776 |  |  |  | 2,133 |
| Lithuania |  |  |  |  |  |  |  |  |  |  | 6,489 | 4,113 |  | 1,512 |
| Luxembourg |  |  |  |  |  |  |  |  |  |  |  |  |  | 56 |
| Malta |  |  |  |  |  |  |  |  |  |  |  |  |  | 2,282 |
| Netherlands/Dutch | 6,358 | 12,559 | 17,177 | 29,410 | 30,406 | 33,471 | 33,499 | 32,128 | 24,722 | 20,215 | 20,259 | 15,095 | 10,633 | 8,669 |
| Norway | 440 | 1,516 | 3,520 | 7,795 | 7,582 | 7,638 | 6,888 | 7,201 | 5,345 | 4,071 | 3,723 | 1,502 |  | 607 |
| Poland | 117 | 974 | 5,421 | 15,669 | 28,286 | 62,419 | 103,926 | 119,228 | 96,826 | 81,595 | 58,061 | 42,499 | 26,968 | 18,634 |
| Portugal | 112 | 31 | 18 | 76 | 10 | 20 | 67 | 131 | 97 | 136 | 322 |  | 150 | 225 |
| Romania/Rumania |  |  |  |  | 11 | 510 | 6,331 | 11,482 | 8,476 | 6,421 | 4,585 |  |  | 5,226 |
| Serbia-Croatia |  |  |  |  |  |  |  |  |  |  | 6,169 |  |  |  |
| Slovakia |  |  |  |  |  |  |  |  |  |  | 5,518 |  |  |  |
| Slovenia |  |  |  |  |  |  |  |  |  |  |  |  |  |  |
| Spain | 11 | 34 | 39 | 61 | 61 | 51 | 441 | 1,341 | 840 | 890 | 1,100 |  |  |  |
| Sweden | 266 | 2,406 | 9,412 | 27,366 | 26,956 | 26,374 | 24,707 | 23,905 | 17,346 | 12,322 | 8,625 | 4,438 | 2,416 | 778 |
| Switzerland | 1,269 | 2,116 | 2,474 | 2,562 | 2,617 | 2,780 | 1,755 | 2,834 | 2,116 | 1,709 | 7,883 | 1,060 |  | 1,294 |
| United Kingdom |  |  |  |  |  |  |  |  |  |  |  |  |  | 602 |
| England |  |  |  |  |  |  |  |  |  |  |  | 44,849 | 33,216 | 23,841 |
| England and Wales | 26,107 | 35,635 | 44,095 | 56,157 | 44,677 | 43,510 | 48,303 | 64,957 |  |  | 158,984 |  | 19,682 | 13,733 |

| | 1860 | 1870 | 1880 | 1890 | 1900 | 1910 | 1920 | 1930 | 1940 | 1950 | 1960 | 1970 | 1980 | 1990 |
|---|---|---|---|---|---|---|---|---|---|---|---|---|---|---|
| Scotland | 5,705 | 8,552 | 120,731 | 12,058 | 10,341 | 9,952 | 13,175 | 35,256 | 49,099 | 42,726 | | | 10,350 | 6,556 |
| Ireland | 30,049 | 42,013 | 43,413 | 39,065 | 20,434 | 16,531 | | | 27,306 | 24,887 | | | 852 | 654 |
| Northern Ireland | | | | | | | | 6,138 | 3,601 | 576 | | | 850 | 326 |
| Ireland (Eire) | | | | | | | | 11,390 | 8,905 | 9,958 | | 10,756 | 12,206 | 10,773 |
| Wales | | | | | | | | | | | | | | 394 |
| Yugoslavia | 17 | 221 | 503 | 170 | 177 | 500 | 94,266 | 16,468 | 12,517 | 11,453 | | | | |
| Other Europe | | | | | | | 3,243 | 6,555 | 5,306 | 7,258 | 11,536 | 26,048 | 13,142 | 7,590 |
| SOVIET UNION/U.S.S.R. | 68 | 194 | 1,560 | 11,889 | 4,138 | 15,822 | 45,313 | 34,348 | | | | 17,134 | | |
| Russia | | | | | | | | | 32,229 | 30,804 | | | | |
| Ukraine | | | | | | | | | | | 8,653 | | | |
| Lithuania | | | | | | | 5,472 | | | | 8,877 | | | |
| Finland | | | | | 18,910 | 31,144 | 30,096 | | | | | | | |
| ASIA | 21 | 61 | 245 | 332 | 652 | 2,061 | 7,632 | 13,242 | 17,471 | 12,566 | | 25,783 | 77,476 | 102,732 |
| Afghanistan | | | | | | | | | | | | | | 68 |
| Arabia | | | | | | | | | | | 5,282 | | | |
| Bangladesh | | | | | | | | | | | | | | 618 |
| Burma | | | | | | | | | | | | | | 102 |
| Cambodia | | | | | | | | | | | | | | 746 |
| China | | | | | | | | | | | 1,516 | 3,026 | 3,615 | 6,036 |
| Cyprus | | | | | | | | | | | | | | 150 |
| Hong Kong | | | | | | | | | | | | | | 1,151 |
| India | | | | | | | | | | | | | 8,879 | 13,386 |
| Indonesia | | | | | | | | | | | | | | 922 |
| Iran | | | | | | | | | | | | | | 2,042 |
| Iraq | | | | | | | | | | | | | | 14,343 |
| Israel | | | | | | | | | | | | | | 1,449 |
| Japan | | | | | | | | | | | | 1,838 | 3,643 | 7,094 |

| | 1860 | 1870 | 1880 | 1890 | 1900 | 1910 | 1920 | 1930 | 1940 | 1950 | 1960 | 1970 | 1980 | 1990 |
|---|---|---|---|---|---|---|---|---|---|---|---|---|---|---|
| Jordan | | | | | | | | | | | | | | 1,987 |
| Korea | | | | | | | | | | | 1,075 | | 7,363 | 8,384 |
| Kuwait | | | | | | | | | | | | | | 376 |
| Laos | | | | | | | | | | | | | | 3,334 |
| Lebanon | | | | | | | | | | | | | | 10,488 |
| Macau | | | | | | | | | | | | | | 699 |
| Malaysia | | | | | | | | | | | | | | 27 |
| Nepal | | | | | | | | | | | | | | 699 |
| Pakistan | | | | | | | | | | | | | | 2,038 |
| Palestine | | | | | | | | | | | | | | 1,312 |
| Phillipines | | | | | | | | | | | | | 7,922 | 9,837 |
| Saudi Arabia | | | | | | | | | | | | | | 702 |
| Singapore | | | | | | | | | | | | | | 255 |
| Sri Lanka | | | | | | | | | | | | | | 131 |
| Syria | | | | | | | | | | | | | | 1,590 |
| Taiwan | | | | | | | | | | | | | | 3,481 |
| Thailand | | | | | | | | | | | | | | 1,576 |
| Turkey | | | | | | | | | | | | | | 1,619 |
| United Arab Emirates | | | | | | | | | | | | | | 63 |
| Vietnam | | | | | | | | | | | | | 3,989 | 4,866 |
| Yeman Arab Republic | | | | | | | | | | | | | | 1,469 |
| West Asia | | | | | | | | | | | | 13,296 | | |
| Other Asia | | | | | | | | | | | | 7,623 | | 170 |
| NORTH AND CENTRAL AMERICA | | | | | | | | | | | | | 94,555 | |
| NORTH AMERICA | | | | | | | | | | | | | | |
| Bermuda | | | | | | | | | | | | | | 109 |
| Canada | | | | 30,445 | 32,483 | 28,083 | 27,268 | 28,530 | | | | 90,696 | 76,612 | 54,630 |
| Canada – French | | | | | | | 18,635 | | | | | | | |

| | 1860 | 1870 | 1880 | 1890 | 1900 | 1910 | 1920 | 1930 | 1940 | 1950 | 1960 | 1970 | 1980 | 1990 |
|---|---|---|---|---|---|---|---|---|---|---|---|---|---|---|
| Canada – other | 36,482 | 89,590 | 148,866 | 150,970 | 151,915 | 143,154 | 1,461,113 | 174,763 | 20,681 | 15,786 | | 7,604 | 9,903 | 13,656 |
| Mexico | 11 | 25 | 14 | 89 | 56 | 82 | 1,268 | 9,739 | 138,567 | 126,472 | | | | 48 |
| Other North America | 17 | 144 | 217 | 227 | 294 | | 671 | | 3,694 | 5,235 | | | | |
| CARIBBEAN | | | | | | | | | | | | | | 6,634 |
| Antigua & Barbuda | | | | | | | | | | | | | | 87 |
| Aruba | | | | | | | | | | | | | | 36 |
| Bahamas | | | | | | | | | | | | | | 258 |
| Barbados | | | | | | | | | | | | | | 157 |
| British West Indies | | | | | | | | | | | | | | 17 |
| Cuba | | | | | | | | | | | | 2,046 | 2,147 | 2,270 |
| Dominica | | | | | | | | | | | | | | 19 |
| Dominican Republic | | | | | | | | | | | | | 285 | 455 |
| Grenada | | | | | | | | | | | | | | 52 |
| Haiti | | | | | | | | | | | | | | 238 |
| Jamaica | | | | | | | | | | | | | 1,655 | 2,084 |
| Netherlands Antilles | | | | | | | | | | | | | | 50 |
| St. Kitts-Nevis | | | | | | | | | | | | | | 73 |
| St. Lucia | | | | | | | | | | | | | | 16 |
| St. Vincent & the Grenadines | | | | | | | | | | | | | | 47 |
| Trinidad/Tobago | | | | | | | | | | | | | | 503 |
| West Indies, not specified | | | | | | | | | | | | | 5,908 | 154 |
| Other Caribbean | | | | | | | | | | | | | | 96 |
| CENTRAL AMERICA | | | | | | | | | | | | | | 2,191 |
| Belize | | | | | | | | | | | | | | 228 |
| Costa Rica | | | | | | | | | | | | | | 275 |
| El Salvador | | | | | | | | | | | | | | 245 |
| Guatemala | | | | | | | | | | | | | | 318 |

| | 1860 | 1870 | 1880 | 1890 | 1900 | 1910 | 1920 | 1930 | 1940 | 1950 | 1960 | 1970 | 1980 | 1990 |
|---|---|---|---|---|---|---|---|---|---|---|---|---|---|---|
| Honduras | | | | | | | | | | | | | | 298 |
| Nicaragua | | | | | | | | | | | | | | 150 |
| Panama | | | | | | | | | | | | | | 609 |
| Other Central America | | | | | | | | | | | | | | |
| Other America | | | | | | | | 1,141 | 1,067 | 2,290 | | | 6,967 | |
| Not Specified | | | | | | | | | | | 24,551 | | 22,971 | 9,893 |
| ALL OTHER PLACES | 27 | 258 | 436 | 635 | 830 | 857 | 1,138 | 1,431 | 1,183 | 1,624 | | 3,212 | | 355,393 |
| All Places | | | | | | | | | | 3,506 | 38,384 | 11,768 | | 9,883 |
| Not Reported | | | | | | | | | | 52,964 | | | | |
| Total | 149,093 | 265,010 | 388,508 | 543,880 | 541,657 | 595,574 | 726,635 | 849,297 | 683,030 | | 782,495 | | | |
| TOTAL POPULATION | 749,113 | 11,840,577 | 1,636,937 | 2,093,890 | 2,420,982 | 2,810,973 | 3,668,412 | 4,842,325 | 5,256,106 | 6,371,766 | | 8,875,068 | 9,262,078 | 9,295,297 |

Appendix D

# Michigan's Ethnic Groups

D etermining ethnicity from census material is difficult and confusing. Terms like race, nativity, and ethnicity are difficult to sort out. In the chart on the following pages, race is the first four categories while ethnicity focuses more on the ethnic group membership. It also must be kept in mind that definitions and numbers are as set forth by the census of that particular year.

| Race/Ethnic/Stock | 1910 | 1920 | 1930 | 1940 | 1950 | 1960 | 1970 | 1980 | 1990 |
|---|---|---|---|---|---|---|---|---|---|
| White | 2,785,247 | 3,601,627 | 466,507 | 5,039,601 | 5,917,825 | 6,566,467 | 7,843,805 | 7,893,278 | 7,759,241 |
| Black/Negro/Other | 17,115 | 60,082 | 169,453 | 209,345 | 442,296 | 728,874 | 1,015,513 | 1,197,177 | 1,289,012 |
| American Indian | 7,519 | 5,614 | 70,800 | 6,282 | 7,000 | 9,701 | 16,854 | 44,762 | 58,667 |
| Eskimo | | | | | | | | 102 | 154 |
| Aleut | | | | | | | | 105 | 113 |
| European | | | | | | | | | |
| Austria | | | 34,792 | 47,938 | 48,933 | 43,675 | 40,730 | | 14,908 |
| Belgium | | | 26,818 | | | | | | 37,442 |
| Bulgaria | 446 | 2,067 | 2,273 | | | | | | |
| Czechoslovakia | 9,839 | 17,005 | 44,602 | 35,345 | 38,833 | 18,475 | 32,176 | | 34,100 |
| Denmark | 150,911 | 17,591 | 20,507 | 16,941 | 16,941 | 15,091 | 11,051 | | 31,778 |
| Dutch and Frisian | 91,363 | 100,295 | | | | | | | |
| Dutch/Netherlands | | | 106,476 | 90,187 | 87,400 | 85,797 | 72,763 | 218,306 | 384,178 |
| English and Celts | 574,397 | 629,660 | 165,848 | | | | | 13,274 | 811,283 |
| English | | | | | | | | 708,594 | |
| Flemish | 79,277 | 16,856 | 18,085 | 13,484 | 13,537 | 12,660 | 12,149 | | |
| French | 77,572 | 94,517 | 74,229 | 63,671 | 54,521 | 45,671 | | 150,062 | 379,594 |
| Finland | | | | | | | | | 83,517 |
| German | 386,896 | 395,502 | 365,263 | 282,543 | 261,173 | 234,183 | 184,192 | 1,714,828 | 2,021,618 |
| Greek | 1,481 | 8,369 | 16,175 | 17,368 | 18,943 | 18,221 | 19,519 | 23,859 | 35,118 |
| Hungarian | | | 40,434 | 47,265 | 50,273 | 45,811 | 39,302 | 48,396 | 71,135 |
| Irish | | | | | | | 117,064 | 272,749 | 692,157 |
| Northern Ireland | | | 23,065 | | | | | | |
| Ireland (Eire) | 26,876 | 57,475 | 60,637 | 47,265 | 52,558 | 34,537 | | | |
| Italian | | | 98,048 | 107,431 | 114,502 | 120,363 | 85,078 | 170,740 | 303,210 |
| Latvia | | | 1,216 | | | | | | |
| Lithuania | | | 20,489 | 19,143 | 20,136 | 21,236 | 16,908 | 12,795 | 25,516 |

| Race/Ethnic/Stock | 1910 | 1920 | 1930 | 1940 | 1950 | 1960 | 1970 | 1980 | 1990 |
|---|---|---|---|---|---|---|---|---|---|
| Litunian and Lettish | 2,899 | 12,022 | | | | | | | |
| Luxembourg | | | 1,243 | | | | | | |
| Norwegian | 16,269 | 17,055 | 23,117 | 19,425 | 18,476 | 16,980 | 12,899 | 19,342 | 42,204 |
| Polish | 130,957 | 251,381 | 320,534 | 293,646 | 278,055 | 255,467 | 214,085 | 400,708 | 656,806 |
| Portugese | 47 | 121 | 239 | 224 | 421 | 587 | | 1,529 | 2,615 |
| Romania/Rumania | 929 | 9,229 | 20,381 | 16,776 | | | | | 17,208 |
| Russian | 1,225 | 23,630 | 75,656 | | 14,518 | 14,359 | | 31,673 | 508,365 |
| Ruthenian | 203 | 3,337 | | | | | | | |
| Serbo-Croatian | 6,466 | 14,818 | | | | | | | |
| Scottish | | | 65,950 | | | | | 59,749 | 148,774 |
| Scotch-Irish | | | | | | | | | 108,529 |
| Slavic, not specified | 217 | 38 | | | | | | | |
| Slovak | 2,841 | 12,776 | | | | | | | 52,683 |
| Slovenian | 5,556 | 6,808 | | | | | | | |
| Spain | 297 | 2,400 | 2,149 | | | | | | |
| Swedish | 61,680 | 66,807 | 68,577 | 52,417 | 58,166 | 44,991 | 33,939 | 53,740 | 117,046 |
| Switzerland | | | 11,066 | 8,474 | 8,576 | 7,642 | 5,442 | 4,383 | 29,186 |
| Turkey in Europe | 305 | | | | | | | | |
| Ukrainian | | | | | | | | | 332,467 |
| United Kingdom | | | | 207,866 | 188,254 | 179,826 | 149,512 | 22,290 | |
| U.S.S.R. | | | | 77,549 | 82,454 | 77,441 | 65,605 | | |
| Wales | | | 6,024 | | | | | | |
| Yugoslavia | | | 33,492 | 27,157 | 28,298 | 30,736 | 30,375 | | 26,314 |
| Other European | | | 7,249 | 35,142 | 43,331 | 46,561 | 94,603 | 1,588,017 | 19,488 |
| Asia | | | | 27,333 | 30,101 | 37,715 | 55,181 | | 65,906 |
| Arab | | | | | | | | | 22,401 |
| Asian Indian | | | | | | | | 15,363 | |
| Cambodian | | | | | | | | | 634 |

| Race/Ethnic/Stock | 1910 | 1920 | 1930 | 1940 | 1950 | 1960 | 1970 | 1980 | 1990 |
|---|---|---|---|---|---|---|---|---|---|
| Filipinos | 49 | 787 | 787 | 139 | 1,517 | 3,130 | 4,953 | 11,132 | 14,571 |
| Japanese | | 184 | 176 | | | | | 6,460 | 10,313 |
| Hmong | | | | | | | | | 2,304 |
| Laotian | | | | | | | | | 2,540 |
| Korean | | | | | | | | 8,948 | 16,689 |
| Syrian | | | 11,760 | | | | | | |
| Thai | | | | | | | | | 1,353 |
| Vietnamese | | | | | | | | 15,363 | 5,404 |
| West Asia | | | | | | 26,590 | 31,579 | 53,856 | 6,646 |
| Other Asia | | | | | | 4,719 | 12,925 | | |
| Subsaharan Africa | | | | | | | | | 9,917 |
| America | | | | | | | | | |
| Canada | | | | 425,338 | 415,338 | 417,228 | 363,154 | | 27,790 |
| Canada-French | | 87,911 | | | | | | | 124,227 |
| Canada-other | | 411,091 | | | | | | | |
| Newfoundland | | | 1,545 | | | | | | |
| Hispanic | | | | | | | 151,070 | 53,884 | 1,431,636 |
| Mexican | | | 1,495 | 2,162 | 4,710 | 24,298 | 31,067 | 107,776 | |
| Puerto Rican | | | | | | | 6,769 | 12,072 | |
| Cuban | | | | | | 1,038 | 3,231 | 3,639 | |
| Other Hispanic | | | | | | | | 34,154 | |
| United States of America | | | | | | | | | 332,467 |
| West Indies | | | 716 | | | | | | 5,989 |
| Central and South America | | | 1,249 | | | 7,688 | 1,339 | | |
| Other America | | | | | | | | | |
| Pacific Islander | | | | | | | | | |

| Race/Ethnic/Stock | 1910 | 1920 | 1930 | 1940 | 1950 | 1960 | 1970 | 1980 | 1990 |
|---|---|---|---|---|---|---|---|---|---|
| Polynesian | | | | | | | | | 1,753 |
| Hawaiian | | | | | | | | | 724 |
| Samoan | | | | | | | | | 168 |
| Tongan | | | | | | | | | 2 |
| Other Polynesian | | | | | | | | | 7 |
| Micronesia | | | | | | | | | |
| Melenesian | | | | | | | | | 63 |
| Other Micronesian | | | | | | | | | 25 |
| Pac Is (not specified) | | | | | | | | | 852,441 |
| All Other | | | 2,893 | 9,996 | 8,450 | 4,203 | 7,129 | | 257,208 |
| Not Reported | | | | | | 15,047 | 40,587 | | 828,160 |
| TOTAL POPULATION | 2,810,173 | 3,668,412 | 4,842,325 | 4,842,325 | 5,256,105 | 7,824,965 | 8,875,068 | 9,262,078 | 9,295,297 |

# Index